THE RAILROAD FORGER
AND THE
DETECTIVES.

"One was a young man of far less rustic appearance than his fellows."

THE

RAILROAD FORGER

AND

THE DETECTIVES.

BY
ALLAN PINKERTON

Black Squirrel Books® 🐿®
an imprint of The Kent State University Press
Kent, Ohio 44242   www.KentStateUniversityPress.com

This facsimile and edition was produced using a scan of a first-edition copy of *The Railroad Forger and the Detectives*. The original edition is part of the Borowitz Collection in the Kent State University Special Collections and Archives and is reproduced with permission.

BLACK SQUIRREL BOOKS® 🐿®
Frisky, industrious black squirrels are a familiar sight on the Kent State University campus and the inspiration for Black Squirrel Books®, a trade imprint of **The Kent State University Press.**
www.KentStateUniversityPress.com

Published by The Kent State University Press, Kent, Ohio 44242
ISBN 978-1-60635-434-6
Manufactured in the United States of America

First published by G. W. Carleton & Co., Publishers, New York, 1881.

Cataloging information for this title is available at the Library of Congress.

25 24 23 22 21   5 4 3 2 1

PUBLISHER'S NOTE

The Kent State University Press

In bringing you these Pinkerton Detective Stories in new facsimile editions, we hope to accomplish several purposes:

- To highlight the breadth and depth of the Borowitz Collection within the Kent State University Special Collections and Archives. These original Pinkerton editions are part of a vast collection of true crime and detective materials, including books, pamphlets, broadsides, and other artifacts. Please visit https://www.library.kent.edu/special-collections-and-archives/borowitz-collection to browse this amazing resource.
- To choose good stories, highlighting the longstanding popularity of the detective genre, particularly in American culture. Both nonfiction and fiction books have a strong hold on our cultural imagination, and these Pinkerton books—like many, but perhaps even more than most—are classified as nonfiction but obviously have a strong fictional component. With the Pinkerton National Detective Agency existing as an ongoing entity, the promotional element of these books cannot really be overstated.

- To add to our understanding of the late nineteenth century, a time of great historical importance in American history. While we must remember that the Pinkerton books have a fictional component, they also represent significant episodes, movements, and attitudes of the late 1800s.

In thinking about this last purpose, in particular, it's important to provide a bit of context. One should keep in mind that the books include racial, ethnic, and gender stereotypes too widely prevalent during this period in history; indeed, some of the language and depictions of individuals are not only unfair but offensive. As all too representative of that time, it's remarkable to see how matter of factly such characterizations are presented. In addition, one must understand that the Pinkerton Agency—in these books presented as the absolute "good guys"—are known to have used underhanded tactics, violence, and even illegal methods as a matter of course. Just a few years prior to the publication of *The Railroad Forger and the Detectives,* for instance, Pinkerton agents worked as infiltrators in the open conflict of the Great Railroad strike of 1877, which left over 100 people dead.

Much has been written about the Pinkertons recently, including fine articles in *Grunge* and *Teen Vogue.* The Agency and its motto, "We Never Sleep," are a part of our cultural consciousness; thus, a look at these books, with all the context and backstory pulled close, is both interesting and instructive.

Happy reading.

EXPLORING THE BOROWITZ COLLECTION

Cara Gilgenbach
Special Collections and Archives, Kent State University

The Borowitz Collection, from which the editions of the Pinkerton detective stories are taken, was officially gifted to Kent State University in 1989 by Albert and Helen Borowitz of Cleveland, Ohio. The collection includes primary and secondary sources on crime as well as works of literature based on true crime incidents.

Albert and Helen Borowitz, both scholars themselves, built a scholarly collection—one that affords more than sufficient breadth and depth to support any number of research inquiries. The Borowitz Collection reflects the multidisciplinary expertise of Albert Borowitz (a Harvard graduate with degrees in classics, Chinese regional studies, and law) and his late wife, Helen Osterman Borowitz (a Radcliffe graduate and art historian with literary interests). In addition to collecting, Albert Borowitz is himself a scholar of true crime, having published over a dozen books and many articles on the topic, most notably his masterwork, *Blood and Ink: An International Guide to Fact-Based Crime Literature*.

The Borowitz collection is an extensive one, documenting the history of crime, with primary emphasis on the United States, England, France, and Germany from ancient times to the present day. It includes groups of materials on specific criminal cases that have had notable impacts on art, literature, and social attitudes. This provides the researcher with a wealth of material on those cases and their cultural effects. The collection includes nearly 15,000 volumes of books and periodicals, complemented by archival and manuscript collections. Special areas of note include an excellent collection of Sherlock Holmes and other Arthur Conan Doyle early editions; nonfiction and fiction works related to Jack the Ripper; nineteenth- and twentieth-century British and American crime pamphlets and broadsides; a Wild West collection; crime-related photographs, playbills, postcards, and other ephemera; and artifacts, graphics, and memorabilia related to crime.

The Borowitz Collection includes numerous works of detective stories, both fiction and nonfiction, including books from the Pinkerton Detective Agency series, which embody the collection's central theme, namely how real-life elements of crime infiltrate creative works and works of the imagination. Although true crime is the primary focus of the Borowitz Collection, it also contains notable holdings in several other topics and genres, including a vast collection of sheet music spanning more than two centuries of popular musical taste and distinguished literary collections.

The collection provides rich sources to users as diverse as crime historians, film documentarians, museum curators, television and radio producers, antiquarian book dealers, novelists, and faculty and students of history, American studies, women's studies, and criminal justice, to name just a few. Kent State University is proud to steward this collection, and the present project to republish the Pinkerton detective stories is a further outgrowth of our desire to make these interesting and informative resources available to a wider audience.

CONTENTS.

PREFACE.

Of the story here given to the light I may speak as of those in the volumes I have already published. The characters with whom the reader will make acquaintance, have all been in the flesh. But few of them, so far as I know, have yet quitted it. The identity of some has been vailed by fictitious names,—but that is out of regard for personal susceptibilities. Any one of those introduced would be able to recognize a faithful account of the events narrated.

For the personal reasons mentioned I have also thought best to disguise certain localities under invented names. None of those substitutions, however, are such as to impair in the least the completeness of the chronicle.

Of the events themselves it will be sufficient for me to state, that they had a wide public notoriety at the time of their occurrence. The slight embellishment which is here given to them is derived from that inner knowledge of motives and movements that pertained to my Detective Agency. Our triumph in bringing to justice the bold criminals depicted in this work only differs in circumstances from scores of successes that we have achieved from time to time.

The reader will notice that at several stages of this remarkable detective operation our theories and conclusions were at fault. I repeatedly found that we had no clue to follow. The criminals had utterly disappeared. Conducting such a search was like a traveler striking out upon a trackless prairie or diving into a trackless forest. Under such circumstances I certainly should have hesitated many times about proceeding further with the operation, both on account of the great expense involved and the absolute want of the faintest clue, had not the General Superintendent of the Adams' Express Company, Henry Sanford, Esq., met me on each occasion with cheering expressions of confidence and encouragement and quite as prompt financial aid.

The fact, however, that the devices I employed, and the skill and aptitude of my agents, enabled me continuously to rectify our course, and conduct it to a victorious issue, is but one more testimony to the merits of my system. The detective methods of past days and other countries, would certainly never be competent to the work which is performed by the modern Detective Agency.

It is natural, of course, in this land of long distance and high prices, that operations of the kind I have here described should quite frequently involve a large expenditure of money. If the pursuer of the criminal can sustain this, as in this operation, the success of his cause, however difficult of accomplishment it may seem, is all but certain; while the extremely rare cases of our failure have invariably been those in which there was a needlessly early default of the "sinews of war." As I have explained, with the corporation that employed us in this operation no contingency arose; and, consequently, from the beginning the capture of the outlaws was a foregone conclusion.

ALLAN PINKERTON.

CHICAGO, ILLINOIS,
    September, 1881.

THE RAILROAD FORGER

AND

THE DETECTIVES.

———◆———

CHAPTER I.

"Desk-room to let."—The New Tenant as a polite and business-like Real Estate Agent.—A Mysterious Departure.

FEW persons who have sojourned in any of our large cities can fail to have seen the announcement of "Desk-room to Let." It is one quite peculiar to trade centers, and is rarely to be met with save in the busiest of business quarters.

However little of interest the sign may have for the ordinary pedestrian, to the detective, like myself, it is often quite suggestive. Most frequently the impulse is to regard the spot with attention, as one in which, as the reporters say, "further developments may be expected."

I would not be understood to mean that all occupants of desk-room are subjects for detective mistrust.

Many very worthy brokers, commission merchants, real estate agents, and casual dealers of various kinds, are limited by necessity to such shreds of office shelter. These are men generally of irrepressible business instincts, but who, having small capital or none, would be the merest pariahs of commerce without their desks. For them it constitutes the local habitation and the name that are essential to relations with the fraternity of trade.

And there are others that I know, men of ample substance, who thus restrict themselves for economy's sake. These are affluent old money-bags, who have ostensibly retired from the cares of business, but who shuffle out at intervals with a plethoric bank-book, to buy a ship, or an estate, or the third of a silver mine. These employ such desks for their temporary seed-sowing, and then, like patient old gardeners, retire into the shade and wait for their plants to fructify.

It is quite a different class from any of these that brings desk-room into the circle of suspected institutions. I now allude to the gentry who use it as a cover for predaceous enterprises,—who live by their incursions into the ever-fat pastures of trust and credulity.

These men hire "desk-room" in some respectable office; they hang out a pretentious shingle, all gilt and blazoned; they transact, or appear to transact, business of more or less importance—and in a few days they are gone again, no one knows whither. In the interval

they have probably sold—for very seldom they buy—
the stock of some flourishing railroad; or shared out,
on paper, the mines of a new Eldorado, or broad
western land-tracts, flowing with milk and honey,
also on paper. Anyhow, they are gone, and few ever
miss them from the ways of commerce, save the dupes
who invested in their rotten schemes, or the detective
who "wants" them on some criminal charge. These,
and their like, make up a large class of the tenants of
desk-room; and with one of their number our story
has principally to deal.

In the latter months of the year 186– this notice of
" Desk-room to Let " was displayed on a card-board sign
at the entrance hall of No. 323 Chestnut Street, Philadelphia. The building was a large one, let out in
separate offices, except that the second floor was occupied entirely by the printing establishment of Mr. E.
M. Grattan. The composition and press-rooms of Mr.
Grattan covered about five-sixths of the area of his
tenement. The remaining space, front, was a small
office, entered by a distinct door from the landing, and
communicating by a rearward door with the printing
rooms.

This office had two windows facing out on Chestnut
Street; and though quite unpretentious in its appointments, was a cozy and pleasant-looking apartment. The
floor was covered with a gayly-striped fiber matting;
some lithographed specimens and pictorial trade cards

hung on the painted walls, and a small fire-proof safe was disposed in one of the corners. In a railed inclosure near one of the windows stood a polished walnut-wood desk, faced with green leather, and a cushioned office chair to match. A larger desk extended from the other window toward the door of the printing room. A medium-sized parlor stove, two or three cane-seat chairs, and a clock, completed the total of office equipment.

At the desk last mentioned was usually to be seen a young gentleman—fair and blue-eyed—named Miller, who officiated with zeal as the printer's book-keeper and order clerk. The other desk, within the railing, had formerly been used by Mr. Grattan himself; but as the young book-keeper had become conversant with his business, its clerical requirements almost entirely devolved upon him, and the larger desk was found adequate for every purpose. Hence was the walnut-wood desk "to let."

About the middle of November a stranger stepped jauntily into Mr. Grattan's office, to ask for information about the tenantless desk. He was a tall, spruce, business-like gentleman, apparently about thirty years of age, and had a pale and somewhat delicate countenance, framed, in part, by short, dark side-whiskers. He was quite genteelly, if not fashionably, dressed, and his pliancy of tone, and air of easy assumption, betokened the native of these sovereign States. The skill with which he expressed and expectorated tobacco-juice, might be reckoned by some observers as an evidence to the same effect.

When the visitor announced his purpose, the book-keeper summoned Mr. Grattan, who chanced at the moment to be in the printing-room. That gentleman at once came forth, tendered the stranger a chair, and then peered expectantly at him through his gold-rimmed glasses. The latter was not long in introducing himself, and, indeed, was almost needlessly explicit in justifying his own purpose.

His name was Cone, he said,—Thomas H. Cone, from Paterson, New Jersey, where he had been in business for several years. He had sold out in October from his latest undertaking, and designed to start a first-class real estate agency in the spring. Some prior business relations with the City of Brotherly Love had induced him to select it as the theater of his new enterprise. Already he had been appointed agent for some nice cottage property, owned by a friend, at Germantown, just north of the city; other agencies had been promised him from the new year; and it was not at all unlikely he should invest some of his own funds in suburban building lots.

All this was rattled off with fluent plausibility, and suggested only to the worthy printer that Mr. Cone was a promising young man indeed, and would make a very successful real estate agent.

" Meanwhile," pursued Mr. Cone, " I have only to watch the market closely, and shall not require a separate office for many months to come. I have concluded that a desk for my correspondence, in some location where I can mature my business plans, will answer all present purposes. Now, your place, Mr. Grattan, is so centrally situated, and so handy to the post-office, banks, and so forth, that when I saw the notice down-stairs I was at once taken with it. If agreeable, therefore, I should like to become your tenant. I shall not be very much in your way, so long as my business is undeveloped, nor shall I have many callers, except, perhaps, the mail carrier and the express-man. Let's see ; which is the desk ? what rent do you ask for it ?"

Delighted at the chance to secure so good a tenant, Mr. Grattan indicated the desk within the railing ; and suggested as a fair rental the sum of ten dollars per month.

Mr. Cone walked over to the desk, opened and shut it, looked down the street, and up at the opposite windows, and stepped back from his review with a pleased expression.

" Well," he said, smilingly, as he took out his wallet, "it is by no means exorbitant in such a nice little office. You may let me have a receipt for the first month's rent, Mr. Grattan, and I can begin my occupancy to-morrow."

At a sign from his employer the attentive book-keeper made out a receipt, which, after counting his ten dollars, was passed to the new tenant. A few courteous remarks about the weather, the prevalent dullness of trade, and such like topics, were next in order; after which Mr. Cone took his leave with a cordial "Good-day."

On the succeeding day the gentleman installed himself in the office, and thenceforth attended with reasonable regularity, principally in the forenoons. He was chatty and pleasant of demeanor, and proved to be quite an agreeable business neighbor. His knowledge of the world and its ways, and a lively manner of discoursing thereon, ingratiated him speedily with the blonde young book-keeper. He also won the heart of the smutty apprentice, or printer's "devil," by the occasional gift of a dime for the purchase of roasted peanuts, said dimes, however, being more frequently invested in the atrocious cigars that are peddled round Independence Hall. To Mr. Grattan himself, whenever that gentleman chanced into the office, Cone would extend a most friendly greeting, and amuse him not a little by some pungent remarks on the topics of the hour. Occasionally he made reference to his own business, and its encouraging prospects, wherein he enlisted still further Mr. Grattan's sympathy, by giving him the order for a small supply of cards, letter paper and envelopes, suitably printed for his business as a real estate agent. These were delivered, and promptly paid for; as was also the month's rent which became due in the middle of December.

If conclusions were to be drawn from the regularity of Mr. Cone's correspondence, his business was indeed full of promise. He seldom came in of a morning without bringing letters from the post-office. These he was wont to set out before him methodically on the desk. With much ostentation he would then examine each communication, and proceed to indite the replies. The folding, enveloping, and addressing of these latter would next be accomplished with like formality; and he always, on leaving, carried his own mail to the post-office. In short, Mr. Cone was precision itself in all his movements; as he was perfect neatness in all his belongings. Not a torn envelope nor spoiled letter sheet was ever left behind after his forenoon's task; while pens, inkstand, paper, and all the rest, were disposed in their proper places as in the " sanctum " of a bank president.

On two or three occasions express parcels containing money came to the office for Mr. Cone, and as this class of remittances are mostly delivered in the forenoon he was on hand to receive them personally. His identification in such cases as " T. H. Cone, Real Estate Broker," was easily effected through Mr. Grattan. He even became slightly known to the Adams' Express agent, through the incidental exchange of pleasant remarks, while engaged in receipting for his packages.

At Thanksgiving, Christmastide, and in the New Year holidays, Cone was absent each time for three or four days. At his return, he made casual allusion to such absences as visits paid to his relatives. Neither the absences or their unsolicited explanations, however, excited any notice on the part of the honest printer. In perfect good faith he had accepted Mr. Cone for what he claimed to be; and his trust was increasing with the duration of the tenancy.

Even when, from the second week of the new year, his absence was more protracted than usual, Mr. Grattan for a time thought nothing special of it, except that his desk rent would be a little delayed. As my readers will learn, however, he might just as well have hung out again the notice of "Desk-room to Let."

———————

CHAPTER II.

A Troublesome Valentine.—A Rogue above the Average.—"Not the slightest clue."

AT the period of which I write, and almost within a stone's throw of Mr. Grattan's office, my Agency in Philadelphia had been several years in operation, and was then, as now, a highly important branch of my detective machinery. It was under the superintendency, as at the present time, of one of my most accomplished aids, Robert J. Linden. From my earliest experience in the profession—and I was the first in this country to organize a National Detective Agency—1 had realized the necessity, for the more certain discovery and effectual pursuit of criminals, of locating permanently, in some of the largest cities, the flower of my resources in detective ability; and time has certainly demonstrated the merits of my plan.

My Agencies are at the centers of speediest communication with all parts of the Union. They maintain a continuous intercourse, both by wire and mail, with each other, and with my Chicago headquarters. Authority and guidance are dispensed to them; to be repaid in tribute of vigilance and effort. And thus, the intelligence received at either of them of a crime committed, and a criminal escaped, gives prompt operation to all the forces at my disposal.

Through these Agencies, also, a most serviceable intimacy—which is only attainable in large cities—is acquired by my special officers with the members, devices and haunts of the criminal classes;—for crime is gregarious, and aims rather to lose itself in crowds, than to hide itself in solitudes.

Mr. Linden, I have said, had charge of the Philadelphia Agency; and I may here also state, that no more alert or faithful gentleman could be found for that important post. Comparatively young in years, he is ripened in intellect, and rich with treasures of observation. His hatred of crime is so genuine as to make the pursuit and capture of law-breakers a positive luxury to him. And woe betide the guilty fugitive in whose tracks he has once engaged himself! Pointer was never so keen, and sleuth-hound never so persistent as he, until he has run down and secured his man.

On the morning of the 14th of February Mr. Linden was seated in the office of the Agency, when a clerk came in to announce a call from Mr. E. Coleman, Superintendent at Philadelphia of the Adams' Express. As for years previously I had transacted the detective business of the company, Mr. Coleman was well known, and at once admitted. The gentlemen exchanged greetings cordially, but the visitor had a vexed and serious air as he sat down, and there was a visible strain in the cheerfulness with which he introduced his mission.

" Linden, I hope you have got through with your Valentines," he said, throwing a folded letter on the table; "I want you to take a peep at that little one of mine."

My superintendent responded to this pleasantry only by a smile; for he readily divined there were graver matters on hand than the love missives of the season. He then took up the letter, which he opened out, and carefully read through to the end.

It was a communication to Coleman from the Treas-

urer of the Express Company, in New York—Mr. J.
S. Babcock—and apprised him briefly that two certain
drafts which he had sent forward for collection on the
10th day of January, and of which the proceeds were
duly remitted to Philadelphia, for account of T. H
Cone, 323 Chestnut street, were now ascertained to
have been stolen from the mails, and negotiated under
forged indorsements.   The drafts were for amounts of
$929.86 and $322.85, and were drawn respectively on
the Metropolitan and Fourth National Banks of New
York.   The treasurer expressed a hope that in paying
over the money to Cone the proper steps had been
taken for his identification ; so that the company might
now look to him—if, indeed, there were such a person
at all—for the reimbursement of its loss.   Mr. Babcock's letter—as though he clearly saw the true state
of affairs—concluded with the remark that if the fellow were caught, the drafts would be on hand to prove
the fact of forgery.

Mr. Linden looked up from the perusal of this
letter, and reflected a moment on its contents.   It
was but a brief pause, however ; for his professional
instincts enabled him to realize at once that this Cone
was a first-class swindler,—one of those gifted plunderers
who sneak at intervals into the world of trade, only to
prey upon it.   Robbery from the mails, forgery of
drafts, and the negotiation of the forged paper, were

indeed a triplet of achievements above the average rogue!

"Your bird has flown, of course?" he tranquilly inquired of Mr. Coleman.

"Flown!" exclaimed the latter, with energy. "I should say he has flown, the scoundrel, and so clean away that I can't find the smallest clue to his where abouts."

"Ah! indeed," was the quiet interjection of Mr. Linden, who was reviewing in thought the contents of the letter.

"No, sir, not a clue—not a particle of a clue." repeated Mr. Coleman quickly, and then he added: "and now, Linden, you know just why I'm here this morning; knowing, as you do, the invariable policy of the company. We must catch and punish this rogue at all cost. I have merely to ask you to find us this T. H. Cone, that we may give him a taste of the State prison."

"Yes, yes," replied Linden, smiling in spite of himself at his neighbor's impetuosity, "we shall catch the fellow no doubt, but we must proceed systematically. You have doubtless called at this address of his, three-twenty-three, Chestnut!"

Mr. Coleman answered in the affirmative, and then hastily repeated to my superintendent the particulars about Mr. Grattan's desk-tenant, that are already known to the reader. It was only within the hour that he had

2

himself learned them, having rushed to the printer's immediately after reading his morning's mail, and thence, without delay, to the office of the Agency.

"So that's all you could learn of Mr. Cone?" inquired Linden, musingly, when Mr. Coleman had ended his recital.

"That's all," responded the latter, with unaffected chagrin. "The simpleton of a printer doesn't even know where the fellow lodged, or lived; he can only recall vaguely some allusions he made to his boarding at a Mr. Lorker's, at Columbia avenue and Twentieth street. It seems, however, since Cone's last absence became prolonged, that he sent his office boy out there to inquire—and, mind you, that was purely out of uneasiness about the rascal's health—but no such person as Cone could be found, and no one in the neighborhood knew such a boarding-house as Lorker's."

"It is plain that we have a shrewd, experienced rogue to deal with," now observed Mr. Linden, "and the worst of it is, he has got a clear month's start of us. However, we must try and pick up the fellow's trail in some way. I propose that we first make a call together in Chestnut street. Have you time to come along?"

"Oh! yes, by all means," answered the express superintendent, "let me see you make a beginning and I shall rest easier. You know what a faith we all have in Pinkerton's."

CHAPTER III.

*A curious little Incident—Only an old scrap of Blotting-paper—
What a Mirror reflected—Slender Threads of Evidence being
delicately followed.*

THE two superintendents at once went out, and
were speedily in Mr. Grattan's office, seated with
that gentleman by the abandoned desk. For a second
time that morning the candid-minded printer was
obliged to recount the history of Cone's tenancy.
Hitherto he had never even dreamed that his promising
young real estate broker could be a swindler in disguise.
As the whole iniquity of the situation was now revealed
to him, he made desperate efforts to remember something useful. He was far too honest a man not to
anxiously desire the recapture of his hypocritical
tenant.

But, beyond what is already recorded, Mr. Grattan
really knew nothing of consequence. He furnished,
to the best of his ability, a personal description of
Cone, which was carefully copied down by Superintendent Linden. But what was the value of a description
supplied from memory, and founded on mere motive-
less observation? Let any of my readers make the
experiment. Write from memory the description of
some intimate friend, one who has no special mark or
defect, and no salient peculiarity to distinguish him

from his fellows. However carefully done, the chances are that in a brief walk through the city he meets a half dozen persons to whom it would equally apply.

The blonde young book-keeper, Mr. Miller, was next submitted to an interrogatory, and with numerous blushes told what he recollected of Mr. Cone. He disclosed nothing new, however, except a curious little incident that pertained to one of Cone's absences.

On the occasion named, he had unaccountably requested Miller to open any parcel that should come to the office for him. It was after New Year's, and a parcel from Trenton was brought in by the money messenger of Adams' Express. The narrator paid the charges, and received and opened the package, but found to his surprise that it contained only railroad time-tables, and no inclosure of pecuniary value. When Cone, on his return, was informed of the circumstance, he glibly remarked that his friend must have forgotten to put the money in; and when writing, he should give him a good "raking up" for it. Two or three days after he exclaimed quite incidentally, "Oh! Miller, I got a check to-day for that fifty dollars that was left out of my Trenton parcel. It was just as I supposed, a stupid blunder." This had occurred shortly before Mr. Cone left.

"Not much blundering about those express transactions," muttered Linden to Mr. Coleman; "they rather look to me like a plan to scrape acquaintance with your officers, and thus pave the way to an easy identification."

Coleman nodded a rueful assent.

With more or less felicity of expression Mr. Miller next attempted his description of the fugitive, but it contained no new points of importance, and was no more infallible than that previously given by his employer.

The professional zeal of Linden was now thoroughly aroused; and he directed his attention to the desk by which they were seated, and which he had learned was Cone's.

"Mr. Grattan," said he, tersely, "let us see if your tenant has left any papers."

The superintendent himself scarce hoped that such would be the case. This forger or mail depredator, or both, perhaps, in one, had doubtless employed his highest ingenuity in covering up his own tracks. A swindler who had displayed such consummate art in the role of legitimate business, and in all the preliminaries to the collection of the forged drafts, would not be wanting in precautions for his ultimate safety.

Mr. Linden looked anxiously, however, into the now opened desk. Its entire contents might have been registered at one glance. There were the cards, letter-paper and envelopes of "T. H. Cone, Real Estate Agent," all primly arranged in their several places. A ruler, mucilage bottle, and such like desk requisites were also visible. But everything was disposed as neatly as in a toy-house—no disorder, no untidiness, no rubbish. And neither written nor printed document, nor stray letter, nor even a torn envelope or discarded scribbling sheet, gave other token that the desk had ever been used.

Mr. Coleman turned away in disgust, while the detective continued to gaze, almost mechanically, over the unpromising field. "Verily," he half muttered to himself, at last, "this Cone was a bright boy; he has indeed gone, and left not a wreck behind."

But suddenly Linden's attention became riveted on one of the articles in the desk, and a light flashed through his mind that had the shimmer of hope in it. Casually regarded, or by a casual observer, the object would have been passed by as unworthy of notice. But in the science of criminal detection there is nothing too mean or trifling to be entirely without significance. Therefore it was that Mr. Linden's attention had been fascinated by a little square of blotting sheet, no larger of surface than a page of note paper. But it was also a much-used piece, thumb soiled and frayed at the edges, and scarred all over with a network of ink-marks.

"I wonder if Cone ever used that thing when writing his letters? Wonder if anything could be deciphered from it? If I could only pick out a name, or an address, from that tangle of ink stains, who knows what it might lead to? I shall certainly have a trial for it, anyhow;" such were the drift and the conclusion of his self-colioquy.

Without daring to give publicity to his hopes, he took up the old blotting sheet, and quietly placed it in the leaves of his pocket memorandum, Mr. Grattan looking on in complete mystification. Having next cautioned the printer and his book-keeper to have nothing to say about this visit and its purpose, the superintendent made a sign to Mr. Coleman, and with him left the office. Arrived at the corner of South Third street he requested that gentleman to excuse him for a while, and promising to confer with him again in the course of the day, turned his steps once more to the Agency.

A few minutes later Mr. Linden had locked himself into his private room, and might be seen—if any were there to see—standing full in the light of the window, and gazing anxiously into a looking-glass which he had suspended from the sash-fastener. But it was no mystery of the toilet, nor prompting of personal vanity that thus engaged him. His was not the taste nor temper to fritter away, on vanities, the time which was demanded for serious duties. Yet never did a belle of society, arrayed for ball-room conquest, regard with more interest her mirrored charms, than did Linden the reflection which greeted him in that looking-glass. It was that of the old piece of blotting sheet from

Cone's desk, which he held upraised in his left hand, almost to a level with his eager eyes. As the crystal surface gave back its labyrinthine inkmarks in their true direction, at least the *elements* of writing became discernible. But oh, in what disorder, in what disheartening chaos ! Upside and down, right side and left, did Linden view the paper, tracing and combining its elusive marks, to gather from their union the letters of a complete word. Several times in succession, beginning at the outside, he managed, with much effort, to group the characters that made part of one word or name ; but the end always baffled him in the blacker confusion near the center of the sheet.

At length, when his eyes were aching with weariness, he began on a fresh series of heavy marks, and clung to them tenaciously across the inky maze. Thus he possessed himself, by painful degrees, of two initials, and a distinct name. Somewhat lower down, and parallel, the word " Ohio " had already shaped itself to his perception ; and his heart now beat fast with anticipations of success.

" Surely," he muttered to himself, " these two lines of writing are related, and are the first and last of a single address ! Their direction, distance apart, style of writing, and relative positions, all seem to betoken the impression from a freshly-written envelope. And that envelope, perhaps, covered a communication to

the forger's family, or a confederate, or—who knows?
—who knows?"

Eagerly, desperately, then, did Mr. Linden begin
his search for the word or words on the presumed
middle line; straining every faculty of mind and
vision to extricate the marks that took the requisite
parallel. And slowly, slowly, but distinctly, one by
one, the letters disengaged themselves, and took order
in his sight. At last he had the material for a completed word, and with an exclamation of mingled
relief and triumph, he rushed from the window to his
desk, and wrote out in great, bold characters—as if
otherwise it might escape him—the following address:

WILLIAM R. WALES,
Redrock,
Ohio.

Not greater, indeed, was the exultation of the old
philosopher, when he won from the murky clouds the
secret of their electricity, than in its own way was
that of my superintendent, over the secret he had
wrested from the reluctant blotting-paper. But the
feeling endured only a few brief moments.

Was it a secret at all? Had it any value, as related
to the forger, Cone? Was this W. R. Wales a living
entity, or a mere myth? And if indeed the former,
would the possession of his address facilitate the search

for the fugitive? Such were the problems that now challenged the investigator.

Well, to one of these doubts, at least, a solution was easily procurable. So Linden telegraphed immediately, in the name of the Express Company, to the agent of the American Express at Redrock, to inquire if a person named W. R. Wales resided in that vicinity; his message being so worded as to suggest merely a difficulty about the proprietorship of some stray parcel.

In an hour from that time the superintendent called over on Mr. Coleman, and found that gentleman wrestling sturdily with the answer to a telegram he had never sent. The mystery was only cleared up for him when Linden narrated his experience with the blotting-paper, and its promising result. Mr. Coleman was delighted with this first installment of success, and said so to my superintendent many times over. The answer of the Redrock express agent had been, that a man named W. R. Wales belonged to that village, but was at present away from home.

A clever detective from the Agency was now dispatched up town, to make thorough search for Cone in the neighborhood where he spoke of having boarded. Nobody knew him, of course, nor any one of his name or description. Mr. Linden also sent a detective to Trenton, and advised the New York Agency to send one to Paterson, each with a mission to hunt up the forger. The former, I will remind my readers, was the city from which Cone received his bogus money parcels; the latter was that in which he claimed to have done business. The superintendent, while directing them, expected but little from either of these searches, and I may anticipate so far as to state, that nothing whatever resulted from them.

The detailed reports of the operation thus entered on were next prepared and dispatched to my New York and Chicago offices. So the day ended.

CHAPTER IV.

Another Series of Felonies discovered.—A Plan of Operations decided upon.

MR. COLEMAN, of Adams' Express Company, as my readers have seen, had been keenly mortified by the intelligence conveyed to him in Mr. Babcock's letter. In a certain degree this mortification was personal; forasmuch as the Philadelphia branch of the company, of which he was the responsible chief, had been used as the medium through which that corporation had been victimized. Not that he had the slightest apprehension that the event would induce any reflection on the administration of his charge; he stood too high in his employers' confidence and esteem for that. No; but he had all the pride of a loyal official in the department under his charge, in the prosperity of the system of which it was a part; and besides, he had the natural indignation of an honest man at seeing his employers plundered—an indignation which in its first impulse might almost have tempted him to do violence to Cone had he met him; and as we shall now learn, this creditable warmth of feeling was destined not to die out from lack of fresh fuel.

The following day came another letter from the treasurer of the company, containing the particulars of such a series of felonies, that he lost not a moment in hastening with the information to my superintendent.

"Isn't this really too bad, Linden?" was all the remark he made, as he flung down the letter on that gentleman's desk.

It was indeed a startling exhibit, and Linden's attention was chained to it from the very opening sentence, which intimated regretfully, that " Cone was not the only forger who had defrauded the express company, nor Philadelphia the only branch at which such frauds had been accomplished."

As early as May of the preceding year, the letter continued, a draft for fifteen hundred dollars was made by a bank at La Crosse, Wisconsin, in favor of Governor C. C. Washburne, and payable in New York at the Bank of North America. Governor Washburne had indorsed this paper over to his physician, who in turn indorsed it to a Boston firm, to whom he remitted it by mail. Although this firm had never received it, the draft was soon after presented for collection at the Pittsburgh branch of Adams' Express, apparently indorsed by them to one R. L. Dudley of that grimy city. Dudley identified in the usual manner, and obtained the fifteen hundred dollars; a loss which reverted to the express company when the paying bank discovered that the indorsement to his favor was an undoubted forgery. When the company began to inquire after Dudley he was found to have left Pittsburgh for parts unknown.

In the September following two drafts were put in for collection at the company's office in Newark, New Jersey, by a man who was known as R. D. Randall, and who, on due identification, was enabled to receive the proceeds. These drafts had both been made in Toledo, Ohio, and were drawn on New York banks, in favor of mercantile houses in Boston. The amounts were five hundred dollars in one case, and one hundred dollars in the other; and the parties in whose favor these sums were drawn, and to whom the drafts had been mailed from the West, were severally prepared to testify, not only that they had never received them, and never indorsed them to such a person as R. D. Randall, but that they did not even know him, and their signatures, as used, were flagrant forgeries. Randall, like Dudley, had since disappeared.

The treasurer had also just learned from the officers

of the "United States" and "American" express companies, that they, too, had been victimized to the extent of several thousand dollars, on drafts from Quincy, Rock Island, and other points west. The features of resemblance with the frauds on the Adams' company were numerous and striking; and sufficiently attested that one and the same gang had been operating in every case. In one of these outside forgeries, which had been perpetrated at Rochester, New York, the swindler had used the name of R. W. Davis.

The leading elements of these swindles were now communicated to Mr. Coleman, wrote the treasurer, because of their similarity with the operation of Cone, and that Pinkerton's—whom he was pleased to learn had been employed in the case—might be armed at all points in their steps toward the capture of that criminal. The authorities of Adams' Express would supply most cheerfully all further information and help that might be requisite, only suggesting now, that as these drafts appeared in every instance to have been stolen from the mails, a friendly co-operation with the post-office authorities might expedite the march of investigation.

Mr. Coleman did not wait to hear Linden's opinion on the disclosures in this grave communication. The general morning duties of his office had still to be attended to; and for several hours to come would require his presence. He therefore took up his hat to depart, saying as he did so, "Linden, you will want a copy of Babcock's letter as one of your campaign documents; I leave it in your care for the present, and shall drop in during the afternoon to hear a little about your plans." Bidding my superintendent "Good-morning," he then went his way.

But so far as its general character and scope were concerned, the plan of my representative had already been decided on. Ere yet he had raised his eyes from the signature at foot of the letter, he had thus concluded to himself: "The best talent and the fullest resources of the National Detective Agency must be at once employed in this operation." In accordance with the requirements of the service he had mailed over-night to my general superintendent at New York, Mr. George H. Bangs, and to myself at Chicago, the history of the Cone forgery, down to the discovery on the blotting-paper. He would now telegraph for Mr. Bangs to come on to Philadelphia, and confer with him minutely on the course to be followed. He would also suggest to him, to first pay a visit in his own city to the treasurer of Adams' Express Company, to obtain the amplest details of the frauds, and tracings, if possible, of the forged drafts.

This step was no sooner decided on than the necessary telegram was dispatched to the metropolis.

The considerations which impelled Mr. Linden to this broad line of procedure may well be reviewed for the enlightenment of my reader. They will render more intelligible the toilsome and expensive detective operations to which it led, and which else might seem disproportioned to the gravity of the case. A like observation will apply to the numerous details concerning the stolen letters and forged drafts, which, at this stage of my narrative, somewhat burden its pages. Their attentive perusal will explain many incidents, and solve a few doubts which might otherwise be detrimental to the interest I would fain create. They are the rough ballasting with which I would prepare the road-bed for safe and pleasant traveling.

CHAPTER V.

A Rigorous and Healthful Business Policy. — The First Feeble Thread of a Net. — Waiting.

A SERIES of audacious felonies, committed at intervals during the greater part of a year, had been carried to their consummation at several of our most prominent business centers. The perpetrators had even assumed the functions and surroundings of honest trade. Their victims, in the cases with which we were specially concerned, were the Adams' Express Company, among the most extensive common carriers in the world. To the care and fidelity of their carrying system, the most important interests of our inland com merce are freely intrusted. Vast quantities of mer chandise and untold thousands in money and valuables, are hourly transported by it between widely distant points. It accommodates, with impartial zeal, the merchant of the populous city and the humblest citizen of the wayside hamlet. The banker of the great metropolis and the least aspiring village grocer alike employ it as the medium of their exchanges ; and so elaborate and necessary has become its service, that, in many parts of the country, its abrupt suspension would occasion, for a time, results somewhat similar to those caused by a trade panic. But the absolute security and integrity of this service are elements of even greater importance than its mere continuance. On this high principle the company themselves have ever proceeded. Nothing that the most watchful super-vision can devise, or the most rigorous exactitude en-force, is omitted from their code of regulations. Promptitude and civility are obligations on all their servants ; unblemished honesty is the *sine qua non.* And, as a corollary to this, neither robbery of their messengers or conveyances, nor fraud nor peculation of their own moneys, have ever been condoned or com-promised by the Adams' Express Company. Nor have they ever spared time, money, or thought on the efforts that became necessary to insure the punishment of any of those offenses. To catch the offender and submit

him to the rigors of justice, make the cardinal point of
their policy in all such cases.

And, if this policy has sometimes occasioned a
seeming loss, in the end it has shown itself to be the
truest economy. The high standard of duty which
inspires it must certainly have its effect on the conduct
of their own officers ; while the stern impartiality with
which it is carried out assures them that fidelity to
their trusts, and not back-stairs influence, is the surest
passport to their employers' favor. Nor should it be
forgotten that this rigid rule of right is otherwise rewarded, through the enlarged measure of confidence
which the public is induced by it to repose in the company.

Now, the patronage with which, in turn, the
Adams' Express Company has favored " Pinkerton's
National Detective Agency," is likewise grounded on
the policy indicated. In my system and its workings
are no such things known as " rewards," or remunera-
tion for services contingent on certain results. My
detective force is an organized ally of the correctional
laws, to be hired and paid for stated operations, as I
am for conducting them to the issue desired. My officers are not accidents, but chosen, salaried associates,
who have therefore no motive either for dalliance with
crime, or favoritism to criminals. And, above all,
being selected as much for sterling devotion to right,
as for vigor of intellect and bravery of person, they are

the prompt and resolute instruments of that law which sanctions their work. In this regard, our efforts as detectives have been the working counterpart of the Adams' company's policy. And thus the relations between the chiefs of that company, and myself and lieutenants, have ripened into regard from identity of principle ; our methods eliciting their warmest approval; their motives challenging our highest esteem.

All these things Mr. Linden knew, if he did not just then review them in detail; and hence it was he had summoned to his assistance my general superintendent.

On the available features of the operations in hand, he also made some reflections entirely pertinent. A number of drafts mailed in the west had never reached the parties to whom the letters were directed ; but instead had been collected on forged indorsements at points in the Eastern and Middle States. Apparently, then, they were stolen from the mails while *en route,* and the thieves should be persons having access to mail matter. The fact that four out of the five drafts reported had originated at Toledo, and the fifth at La Crosse, Wisconsin, located the domain of theft either in the former city, or on the mail routes eastward therefrom. The whole field for detective investigation would therefore be between the branch agencies and the Chicago headquarters. So far, well, thought Mr. Linden.

Again, regarding the case of Cone as a type, there should be confederate forgers outside, to whom this mail thief, or thieves, had passed the stolen drafts. With such confederates, no doubt, lay the crime of forgery, and the felonious utterance of the drafts on the express company. Now, Cone was one of these; that, at least, was clear.

But did Cone, Randall, Dudley, and Davis constitute a gang of confederate forgers?

Probably.

Or were they all one person under these several aliases?

Quite possibly.

Was the W. R. Wales of Redrock, to whom Cone had written, the mail robber in the case?

Improbable; for if he were employed in the mail service, the express agent at Redrock would doubtless have mentioned the fact.

Was he, then, another member of this gang of forgers?

Not unlikely.

And, if neither of these, would the possession of his address assist us in discovering the actual criminals?

"Yes, that it shall," said Mr. Linden to himself, confidently, as he paced his room at the Agency; "it is but the first feeble thread of a net, but of a net which we shall yet weave strong enough to enmesh these plunderers, one and all."

Reserving all further doubts and deductions for the conference with the general superintendent, Mr. Linden proceeded to do what in him lay toward mining the outworks of this citadel of mystery. Every moment lost would now be a gain to the fugitive swindlers. He telegraphed to my son, R. A. Pinkerton, who is superintendent of the New York Agency, to dispatch at once a trusty officer to Newark, to find what could be learned of R. D. Randall. The detective so engaged was to obtain a minute description of that forger from the express company's officers, and give a copy to Mr. Bangs on his departure for Philadelphia.

To the agent of the company at Pittsburgh—a Mr. J. R. Snively, as Coleman informed him—he also telegraphed for some account of Dudley, the forger who had flourished by the Alleghany river. A full description of his person was also asked for, and it was impressed on Mr. Snively that his letter would be looked for in the morning's mail.

Mr. Linden next made inquiries at the post-office about the routes by which mail matter came eastward from Ohio, and on such other points as might serve to furnish light.

And so having done, the superintendent waited.

CHAPTER VI.

*Narrowed Down to one Man.—Desirability of Securing the Co-
operation of the Post-Office Department.—Actual Operations
Begun.*

IN compliance with the telegraphic summons of Mr.
Linden, Mr. Bangs reached Philadelphia about
noon of the following day. His arrival at the agency
may be regarded as the veritable beginning of the pursuit of the forgers. It is true that Linden had made
a notable step forward in discovering even a trace of
the sly-footed Cone. He had likewise initiated, most
creditably, the general course of investigation.

But the wide field of criminal mystery lay dark and
untrodden beyond. Mail-robbers, forgers, and utterers
of forged drafts--of each, one or many—had safely
accomplished their villainous schemes; and, shielded
by an incognito that seemed impenetrable, were still at
large, feasting and rioting, perhaps, on their ill-gotten
spoils. And for all key to their identity, all clue to
their whereabouts, it was only known that at some time
within three months, one of their number had possibly
corresponded with a certain resident of an obscure
western village, who was quite as likely to prove a
guiltless stranger as a guilty accomplice. Deftly indeed had the rogues done their work.

But, build it of whatever material, and however

cunningly, the stronghold of crime is but a house of straw. The keenness of honest intellects was now to be measured against the craft of knaves. The courage and persistence of upright men were now to compete with the recklessness and irresolution of fugitive law-breakers. And bearing in mind what the great dramatist assures us, that

" Thrice is he armed that hath his quarrel just, "

who need fear for the issue of the contest ?

In the first of this series of detective stories, in recounting an operation wherein he was brilliantly serviceable, I took occasion to mention that my general superintendent was " a man from the ranks." Mr. Bangs, indeed, is a gentleman who has risen to the heights of his profession, and won the spurs of his chieftaincy, entirely by the force of his own character. At the time of which I write, as yet to-day, he was a man of indomitable and tireless energy, generously gifted with

" The keen spirit
That seizes prompt occasion,—makes the thought
Start into instant action, and at once
Plans and performs, resolves and executes. "

When I first encountered him he was but a raw young New Englander, with limited knowledge of men, and less of criminals and the world of crime. He had great natural talents, however, and a thoroughly disciplined and loyal mind—faithful to the task of the hour as a sentinel on his post, and resolute, even in small things, to do everything well. A frank and engaging demeanor, readiness of speech and apprehension, a keen eye for what men miscall trifles, and liberal powers of analysis and induction, likewise had their share in his success as a detective. And, in the years of far-reaching experience which he has since had with my Agency, these various qualities have but ripened and intensified, each after its kind, until he who among his friends is the very type of amiability, is dreaded by law-breakers as the phantom of retributive justice !

Before leaving the Empire City Mr. Bangs had made calls on Treasurer Babcock, and General Superintendent Henry Sanford of the Adams' Express Company. From the former he obtained all available particulars, with accurate tracings, of the drafts collected by Cone, Randall and Dudley. From Mr. Sanford, with a hearty wish for his success, he received the stereotyped commission of the company, to spare no time or reasonable outlay in bringing those swindlers to the bar of justice. Through the good offices of the latter gentleman he also obtained from the United States Express Company, for purposes of comparison, a tracing of the forged draft by which R. W. Davis had defrauded them at Rochester.

With so much of dry, but needful preliminary, the reader will now be desirous to step into the room at the

Philadelphia Agency, where my superintendents, Messrs. Bangs and Linden, and Mr. Coleman of the express company, are seated in conference over the multiplied forgeries. Before them on the table are spread out the draft tracings brought from New York, and the other documents pertaining to the case. Of these, Messrs. Bangs and Linden have already made a joint survey, and compared notes and deductions. There is no waste of time, therefore, in useless routine.

"Gentlemen," spoke Mr. Bangs, taking some of the papers in his hand, "we have here the reports of the officers sent out to hunt up Cone, in this city, and at Trenton and Paterson, New Jersey. As you are aware, he has not been heard of; and I think he is not very likely to be through any clue that he has wittingly left behind him. It was highly judicious, however, to begin with these searches, and I congratulate friend Linden on his promptitude."

Mr. Linden bowed his acknowledgments, and the speaker continued.

"Well, we learn from Mr. Babcock's letter that the other swindles on the company were effected at Newark, and at Pittsburgh; and from these points we have descriptions of the men Dudley and Randall, who perpetrated them. I find that though differing from each other, and from Cone's description, in many particulars, they have still so many others in common, as to suggest the identity of all three forgers in one

3

man. And it's altogether probable, indeed, that the
description of this Rochester man, Davis, which we
expect from the other company, will be found to con-
form to them in a like degree. Such a matter as the
precise shade of hair, Mr. Coleman," and here the
superintendent regarded the attentive expressman,
" or trim of whiskers, is of very small account when we
have the height, age, and general appearance in tolerable agreement. Even the fact here reported to us,
that Randall had a front tooth missing, would rather go
to show that the fellow is an adept in disguises.
Detectives only are aware what a great disguise can be
effected, and frequently is, by the use and displacement
of one or more false teeth. But if there were any
doubt whatever about these several swindlers being
one and the same, it seems to me to be set at rest by
the handwriting, as we find it here in the tracings of
the drafts. I think you will both agree with me that
these indorsements of Cone, Randall, Dudley and
Davis have all been written by the same hand."

A re-inspection and comparison of the traced
signatures here ensued, when it became the unanimous
opinion that there was really but one forger. Mr.
Bangs now raised a difficulty for himself, only to brush
it away again.

" It is true," he said, " that the forged indorsements
of the business firms are in different styles of writing ;
but there, you see, variety alone was necessary, the

paying banks in every instance being in a different city from those firms, and quite unlikely to be familiar with their signatures. Any friend of the forger's, if he were not good enough penman himself, could have made those indorsements."

"I should judge he wasn't much of a penman, any-how" grimly observed Mr. Coleman.

"No; it is a streaky, nervous kind of scrawl," replied Mr. Bangs, " but that only makes more remark-able the fellow's intellectual capacity. However, so far as the forgeries are concerned, all this seems to narrow our field down to one man. Of this man, whose name of Cone will suit as well as any other, we only know for a certainty—through Mr. Linden's clever discovery on the blotting-sheet—that he has addressed some kind of communication to one W. R. Wales, of Redrock, Ohio. This Wales, we learn again, is just now absent from his home; but I imagine our very first step should be to send a detective to look after him. By that means alone can we determine whether he is criminally associated in these frauds."

Mr. Coleman concurring in this step, the general superintendent inquired of Linden what officers were disengaged at the Agency?

"Not one except Thomas," was the reply; "the rest are all busy on local operations."

"But Thomas is just the man," said Mr. Bangs; " resolute, noiseless, and quick as a mousing cat. Be so kind as to have word sent to him that I wish to see him in a little while."

This was promptly done through the speaking-tube that communicated with the chief clerk's desk, in the outer office.

"However," resumed the superintendent, almost without a pause, "while we are looking after this forger through the only clue as yet apparent, we must not lose sight of the chance that he may even now be located in some other city, and preparing to play the same game of fraud as before. It seems to me therefore, friend Coleman, that you should write to your chief, Mr. Sanford, and advise the issue of a circular letter to all the agents of the company, describing the methods of this swindler, and furnishing the descriptions of his person already obtained. In that way the various branches will be placed on the alert, and if the fellow should venture to repeat his operation at any of them, not only will he fail very conspicuously, but drop into our hands without more ado."

"I shall write to that purpose this very day, sir," said Mr. Coleman, "and I have no doubt in the world that Sanford will act on your suggestion."

"And now, Coleman," said Mr. Bangs, with more deliberation, "we are confronted by another aspect of this case, which may involve some tedious diplomacy. Our duty to the Adams' Express Company, as detectives, is sufficiently clear. We must capture, if possible, the forgers who have swindled it. You are, so to speak, our clients in this case. But these losses have only fallen on your company, since you were found to have been the unconscious instruments of fraudulent money collection. In the first instance they fell upon the persons who mailed the drafts, and on those to whom they were addressed, and properly payable. Both of these classes had property rights in the violated letters. Of such rights, the post-office is, by law, the constituted guardian. When letters once mailed have been purloined or tampered with, the aggrieved owners become *its* clients. The senders, and should-be recipients of those letters, would naturally apply to the post-office authorities as soon as they realized their loss. The latter, it is quite certain, would begin an investigation as to how they had come about. The very first step of such investigation would be to establish the fact that the letters were really put in the mails. This being ascertained, they would proceed by their own methods to search for the thief within the department. Do you perceive?"

"Certainly, certainly," answered Mr. Coleman, "their activity in such cases is a matter of notoriety."

"Well," resumed the superintendent, "in this search they are probably now engaged. This is why Mr. Babcock, in the letter before us, suggests co-operation with them. He assumes very properly that they are in possession of the preliminary facts. They may

even now be on the track of the thieves; and at all
events, there can be no doubt that whatever information they possess would be of immense value to us."

"Not a doubt in the world about it," interposed
Mr. Coleman.

"But there's just the rub," continued Bangs.
"Like all governmental departments, the post-office is
jealously administered; and more so than any other,
perhaps, on account of the constitutional sacredness of
its trust. The best we can attempt, then, is to show
its authorities how desirable, to *them*, is our co-operation
in this case. It is plain that the forger whom we
specially seek must be a confederate of their mail-thief,
and that the mail-thief whom *they* seek, has an accomplice in our forger. The capture of either one will
almost certainly insure that of the other, but especially
the capture of our forger, for the mail employees are
all well-known, and any who would then show signs of
flight could be pounced upon immediately. On the
other hand, if the mail-thief were the first to be arrested, the inevitable publicity would be a warning to
the forger, and he might escape from the country ere a
pursuit could be organized."

"He certainly would, sir," observed Mr. Coleman,
sadly.

Mr. Bangs went on: "Now, such an escape would
be deplored by the post-office authorities as much as
by ourselves, the prime object of both parties being

the vindication of the laws. I shall endeavor, therefore, to impress upon them that a harmonious plan of action and a simultaneous arrest of the criminals will best subserve the end in view. I think my friend, McPhail, of the Post-Office Special Service at Washington, will not hesitate to extend his good offices in the matter. If he should only give us an introduction to his subordinate in Chicago, who looks after depredators in the north west, Mr. Pinkerton himself could confer with that gentleman, and operations on both sides would be greatly expedited.

Mr. Coleman expressed unqualified approval of this course ; and soon after retired to permit the detectives to work out their plans. Mr. Bangs at once wrote to Washington, and then telegraphed to me a brief synopsis of his action, and of the intention to send officer Thomas to Redrock, Ohio.

The detective was next called in, and directed to inform himself, from the papers on the table, of the merits of the task on hand. This he carefully did, making copies of the personal descriptions, and full memoranda of such dates, names, and other particulars as he thought might prove serviceable. The general superintendent next gave him an idea of his own views of the case ; and such hints as he thought necessary on the subject of shadowing Wales. He was then desired to hold himself in readiness for his western trip, pending the receipt of my telegram approving its purpose.

The latter reached Philadelphia within a very short time, with an order to the detective to await dispatches at Pittsburgh, should further instructions be deemed necessary by the morrow. Mr. Thomas accordingly took the evening express on the Pennsylvania railroad, and by midnight he was far over the rich valleys of the Keystone State, bowling towards the slopes of the Alleghanies.

The correspondence entailed by this operation engaged Mr. Bangs until the following afternoon; but this will be noticed in the order of its results. For the present, at least, my readers will find interest in flitting westward with the "shadow," a term which is applied to the officer who watches and reports the movements of a suspected person; or of any person, indeed, whose movements are of consequence to a detective operation.

CHAPTER VII.

Mr. Pinkerton's Early Experiences in Northern Ohio.—The Village of Redrock.—Detective Thomas as an Interested Mineralogist.

IN meditating over my work that evening at headquarters, I concluded that the time was really opportune for a detective to proceed to Redrock. The dispatches that had thus far reached me were necessarily too brief to admit of a full judgment in the case, but it was clearly the proper thing to look after the man whose name had been found on the forger's blotting sheet. The reported fact, also, that this man was temporarily absent from home, seemed to offer a good chance to quietly investigate his antecedents and surroundings.

But having circulated much in earlier years through the northern portions of Ohio, I was aware that the line of the Yarmouth and Sycamore Valley Railway—on which Redrock appeared as a station—had opened up to settlement a comparatively new region. I had known it as a wilderness of swamps and forests; and time and again have I traversed its dreary solitudes, the Nemesis of some desperate criminal. In those days, as I well remembered, I was often only too happy, after several hours' riding, to come across the nameless clearing whose few scattered houses bespoke a prospect of refreshment and information. Many of these forest clearings had, of course, grown up into villages, and some of them I had heard from as being bustling towns; but I judged that the neighborhood of Redrock must be still sparsely settled, and might be a risky kind of place for a stranger to display inquisitiveness.

On the night of Mr. Thomas's departure, therefore, I sent a telegram for that officer to Pittsburgh, directing him to approach his task with every precaution, and to quarter himself in Yarmouth—which is a thriving Ohioan city some distance westward from Cleveland —until he had devised some pretext for frequenting the village. That my dispatch had reached him, and that its purpose was appreciated, I knew, on the second morning after, when a telegram reached my office announcing that Mr. J. R. Thomas had arrived at Yarmouth, and was staying at the Forest Hotel, near the depot of the Sycamore Valley Railroad.

It was a comparatively easy matter for the detective to obtain at Yarmouth such general information as might serve him for a stepping-stone. He was therefore enabled to transmit to the Agencies the following particulars, by the very first mail after his arrival.

Redrock was a village that had but one door of communication with the eastern part of the Union; and that door was Yarmouth. Its population might consist of about four hundred persons, whose homes and holdings were scattered over a territory nearly two miles square. A few years before the place was without form and void, but the sapient legislators at Columbus had erected it into a corporate village, in the persuasion that it was a most happy conquest from the primeval wilderness, with the manifest destiny of a " center of production." This fond belief had originated among some shrewd farmers, whose homesteads were situated along White Creek, a tributary of the river Maumee, that tumbled westward through a stony dell about half a mile back from the original clearing. The rock formation here consisted mainly of a bluish limestone, with occasional partings of dark-colored shale, or slate, which somebody had averred was the near neighbor of a coal vein. It was certainly of a bituminous character, and the traditions of the first settlers had it, that the Indians in those parts had been seen to use coal in their camp-fires. At all events, it was an argument for the aforesaid farmers, who kept saying: "Now, if we only had a village charter, and a railroad depot and post-office of our own, capitalists would locate among us and quarry out those stone banks. Some of them would be sure to strike the coal-bed, too, and then our lands would greatly raise in value, and the village become a busy and prosperous place." Through the energy of the local representatives, these and such like arguments prevailed in time; and the legislature conceded an elaborate village charter. Very soon after the railroad company established a depot, and the government shed dignity on all by erecting Redrock into a separate post-office. With a neat little wooden church, three drinking saloons,—of which one called itself a hotel—and its firm, abiding faith in a coal-bed, the village seemed now in the path to distinction.

But the expected capitalists didn't locate "worth a cent." As many as four or five quarries were opened and worked a brief while, only to be abandoned in turn as unprofitable. The transportation of the stone to a market proved to be too costly; and quarry labor was dear, when the right kind was at all procurable. The Irish and German laborers who had been imported to the quarries, were many of them at work among the village farmers; while a few still delved and blasted at a solitary stone bank, for the behoof of a Cleveland builder, who only kept working it for a chance to sell out. The much debated coal-bed had never cropped out at all; and farm lands in the neighborhood were still cheap, and farming a remunerative occupation.

Thus much incidentally, and much more that was irrelevant, did Mr. J. R. Thomas learn in a conversation with a land-agent named Stanley; whose card in the Yarmouth *Tribune* had informed him that he held "farm lands for sale on the line of the Sycamore Valley Railway." Nor did it once occur to the land-agent, that though his visitor was somewhat indiff rent to the merits of the soil at other points on the line, he was al. attention when anything was said about the productive region of Redrock. Indeed, to inform himself of the topography and history of that village, the detective had to endure a like tedious chronicle of several other villages westward along the same line. But at length an idea struck him, and he ventured on a direct question.

"Did you say, Mr. Stanley," he inquired, "whether either of these Redrock farms on your list contained a section of the stone ridge?"

"Yes, sir; the larger farm, which is about two-thirds

cleared, extends along the bank of the creek, and has an open quarry on it. Its owner, Mr. Reuben Clark of this city, was one of those who invested in Redrock lands entirely for sake of the stone. But he speedily tired of digging out a building material for which there was no profitable outlet. The smaller parcel of land is a choice clearing, low down in the village, adjoining the homestead of Mayor Wales."

"How!—you don't mean to say there's a mayor at Redrock?" exclaimed Mr. Thomas, who had here chanced on the very name that occupied his thoughts.

"Oh! yes; I thought I told you," returned the land-agent. "The charter of the village provides the whole framework of a municipal government—mayor, trustees, town clerk, and all. The mayor is an excellent old gentleman, too, and is likewise the justice of peace for the district."

"A man full of years and honors, I suppose," observed Mr. Thomas, in an absent-minded manner, but not without a purpose of provoking a reply.

"Yes, sir; Mr. Wales is a highly respected person," pursued Mr. Stanley, "and is regarded as a well-informed, progressive man, and a good neighbor. There's not another resident of the village has the interest of the locality more at heart, or would do as much to accommodate a new settler, as would the mayor himself."

But it did not suit Mr. Thomas to exhibit any special interest in the Wales family, so he merely observed :

"Ah—well—you said that your principal, Mr. Clark, had failed to make the slate-bed pay ?"

"No; not precisely, sir; it was the building-stone he was interested in; the slate, I believe, was never thought much of at any of the quarries."

"Indeed! Now, Mr. Stanley, do you know, I think those gentlemen have made a grand mistake! I have noticed that the shales in a limestone formation are nearly always good enough for flagging purposes; and sometimes capable of being highly polished, so as to serve for mantel slabs. There are certain grades of them, too, which become quite valuable in the manufacture of mineral paint; and others again which——"

"Why, I declare, sir," interrupted Mr. Stanley, "for a farmer you are quite a mineralogist!"

"Not much, sir," answered Mr. Thomas, modestly; "however, my inquiry about the farm lands is on behalf of a brother of mine who has a homestead near Sandusky, but wants to come a little further west. The interest I take in these quarry matters is entirely that of an amateur."

"Well, sir, your brother couldn't easily find a nicer place to locate in than Redrock," now reasserted the land-agent, whose thoughts ran mainly towards the earning of a commission.

"I dare say, Mr. Stanley; I shall certainly make a run over to the village, and write to him fully on all points.

When I hear what his views are, I shall drop in to see you again."

"Do so, sir," urged the communicative land-agent, "and let me hear from yourself what you think of the quarry prospects."

The exchange of a friendly "good afternoon" put an end to the long interview.

"The slate," said Mr. Thomas to himself, as he walked back to the Forest Hotel, "the slate's the thing with which I'll catch the conscience of—of—Redrock!"

CHAPTER VIII.

At the Quarry.—Rody Maguire, the jolly Irish Foreman.—The Detective feeling his Way.

EARLY the following day, Operative Thomas went out by the western accommodation train to Redrock. Without loitering or speaking to any one, he left the little depot, and at once took his way along an ungraded street, east of the village thoroughfare, which he surmised from its course must lead towards White Creek. The supposition proved correct; for after he had passed some gentle acclivities, dotted here and there with dwellings, he came full in view of a bend in the stream where it wriggled along through a narrow channel, flanked on either side by jagged ice. Close to the edge of the creek the street diverged into two lateral roads, the branch to the left leading to a wooden bridge which carried out northward the line of the village main street. The other branch, running east, was furnished for some distance with a rude tramway, and was strewn with such stony refuse as indicated the neighborhood of a quarry.

Along the latter road the detective picked his steps for about a quarter of a mile, being greeted during his progress by the music of drill sledges, heard from a point at which workmen were preparing for a blast. The latter were but three in number, and were engaged on the scarped face of a limestone bluff, one holding the rock drill, and the others, in turn, swinging the heavy sledges. Observing that they had seen him, Operative Thomas advanced more slowly, examining from time to time some broken pieces of stone which he picked up along his path. His interest in these fragments, however, was rather more affected than genuine; for he was also pondering seriously how best to address the workmen.

Suddenly, on rounding a ledge by the roadside, the detective came upon a small wooden hut, used as a toolhouse, before which was seated on a stone block a man who was occupied in the manipulation of blast charges. As he was within a few feet of him there was no further time for reflection, so Thomas saluted him promptly with a "Good day, neighbor!"

As he was within a few feet of him, there was no further time for reflection.

" The same to yourself very kindly, sir," was the civil reply of the quarryman, delivered in a frank and hearty voice, every tone of which was an echo of the Green Isle.

" Is this Mr. Reuben Clark's quarry ?" next inquired the detective.

" No, sir ; that it isn't," was the answer ; " bud it's Misther Andherson's ov Dayfiance—though they say it'll soon be somebody else's. If you're lookin' for Clark's place it's jist beyant the creek brudge a bit."

" I suppose there are some men working over there?" pursued Mr. Thomas ; " I am anxious to get a little information about the stone."

" Arrah ! not a sthroke o' work was done there this six months, sir—an' it's a marcy if we're not all workin' the same way afore long! But sure I can tell you meself a'most anythin' you want about the primeses, an' heartily welcome."

" Thank you, thank you ; but I intend to make an inspection of it as well. Is the rock much the same as what Mr. Anderson has here ?"

" Musha, thin, it's exactly the same," said the Hibernian, " only it's a good dale betther. It's a kind ov limestone, too, bud it's close an' stiff, an' if I was a buildher, I'd rayther have it than any quarry on the creek. But if I may make so bould, sir,—war you thinkin' ov runnin' it ? "

" Well—I can't precisely say," replied Mr. Thomas,

"a friend of mine along near Sandusky is interested in certain kinds of stone, and will quarry extensively if he can only find enough of the right sort. He wants a—"

"Hould on a minute, sir," interrupted the quarry-man; "I see my min is ready for this blast, an' if you only wait till I fix it, I'll take a sthroll over to Clark's place an' show it to you."

Thomas nodded his thanks, while the active fore-man—for such he was—selected the proper charge, put his implements and material carefully away, and went to perform the necessary operation. This having been done, he directed his men under cover, and firing the slow-match himself came hurriedly back to where the detective awaited him. The distance to this point being a safe one, both remained still to observe the result. In about two minutes more the fuse had burnt down, there was a slight tremor of the earth, and the blast exploded with a thundering noise which rever-berated along the creek, and through the dismal forest patches, until the leafless trees seemed to shiver with affright.

"Begorra, that's a stunner!" exclaimed the quarry-man, approvingly, as he distinguished the huge pile of rock fragments that came crashing down through the smoke of the blast.

"There's plinty o' time now, sir, to have a peep at Clark's quarry," he added; at once turning into the way by which Thomas had come.

"I shall be wrong to take you away from your work?" suggested the detective, inquiringly, to his obliging conductor.

"Don't be wan bit onaisy, sir," answered the latter; "my min has their work cut out for 'em, an', besides, we're all takin' things purty cool over here, bekase of Misther Andherson goin' to sell out."

"Then your quarry is about to change hands?"

"So far as I can larn, it is, sir; an' whin that happens, there's one of us at laste 'll be his own boss."

"No doubt you mean yourself," said the detective, in tones of sympathy; "don't you expect to be continued in charge of the work?"

"Divil a wan hour, sir, if it's the man buys it that they say is talkin' about it—a son of ould Jidge Wales he is—though I knows more about takin' out stone, an' handlin' a gang o' min, than any boy around Redrock."

Once more had Mr. Thomas stumbled on the man he was interested in; but though much pleased thereat, he did not lose sight of his instructions to "make haste slowly."

"I suppose," he observed, after a while, "I suppose you are afraid that the new proprietor will tackle his own quarry work?"

"No, it isn't that ayther, sir. Willie Wales, indeed, he's too much of a young squireen for that! But he has a brother in these parts that's not makin' much of his little farm, an' by the way he hangs round the stone banks, an' watches the dhrillin' an' blastin', I think he's layin' himself out for the new job If your own frind tuk it into his head to buy Clark's place, do you think he'd want a foreman, sir ?"

As this diplomatic feeler was put out, the pair had reached the bridge, below which, on the main street, Mr. Thomas descried one of the drinking saloons at which Redrock slaked its thirst. Making an encouraging an-swer to his guide, he also added the happy remark that the day was quite chilly, and a glass of something warm would fortify them for their quarry inspection.

"Bedad, it'll do no harm, sure enough, sir ; though meself dhrinks but little, seein' its not offen I meet wid a gintleman that's so liberal about it."

With this naive explanation from the quarryman Thomas led the way into the saloon, and ordered a couple of hot whisky punches. These were drank in comparative silence ; but under the softening influence of a second glass, his companion thawed out into such voluble friendship, that it became necessary to warn him that "the quarry matter must be kept dark." A confidential wink was the loyal response, and the pair soon left to proceed across the bridge.

"Sure enough, sir," burst out the Irishman, pursu-ing the lead of his own reflections, "you may tell your frind in Sandusky there isn't a boy in this part of Amerikey knows more about quarryin' limestone than

Rody Maguire—though it's himself that says it, that never bragged out of himself yit!"

"So you think it is the intention of this Willie—Willie—what do you call him?—to—"

"Wales is the name, sir," volunteered Rody.

"Ah! yes,—I remember; you think he intends to make his brother foreman of the quarry?"

"Well," answered the quarryman, with philosophic gravity, "it's hard to tell what a man intinds to do until he does it; but there's some very daycent people says that it won't last very long, anyhow—that no matther what the same man puts his money into, he'll nayther have luck nor grace wid it!"

"You don't say!" exclaimed Mr. Thomas. "Can't the gentleman dig out stone and get as good a price for it as any other quarry owner?"

"That's all very thrue," rejoined Rody, "but there's a knowledgeable old sayin' about money, that 'the divil's wages is soon spint'; and by all account the money that's to buy Andherson's quarry was never earned be honest sweat!"

"Mr. Wales is not a man of property, then?" threw out the detective.

"Property!" echoed Rody, with a disdainful emphasis; "sure it's only a twelvemonth ago I saw him wid me own eyes loafin' around the village here, not doin' a hand's turn, and he hadn't the price of a lager beer, only what his old man gev him. An' now, sir, it's nothin' but kid gloves an' goold watches wid him, an' cigars and dhrinks for every one he comes acrass."

"He may have started some profitable city trade?" suggested the considerate Thomas.

"Whatever kind of a thrade it is, sir, he keeps goin' and comin' from some place down aist, stoppin' a few days at a time, an' as sure as he comes back they say he has lashins o' fresh money! Maybe you've heerd tell, sir, what *Keero* and *fano* is?"

Thomas could scarcely suppress a laugh as he discerned in the misplaced syllables the material for the words "Keno" and "faro."

"Oh! yes;" he answered, "I believe they are some plundering games carried on in the big cities."

"I knew be the sound a'most there was nothin' good about *thim*," said Rody, shaking his head impressively; "an' sure I overheerd him myself talkin' to wan ov the young bucks down at Kramer's, an' laughin' about some wan he saw thryin' to 'break the bank'— jist as onconsarned, sir, as if there wasn't the laste bit of harm in it."

Thomas recognized here another common phrase from the gamblers' vocabulary; but he merely lifted up his brows with an expression of virtuous astonishment.

"Yis, sir," continued Rody, by way of explanatory finish, "I've no gridge again any man, nor I don't like to spake bad of any one; but sure ould Jake Bartlett, the tinsmith, that knows every bird ov the Wales family

—an' be the same token there's no love lost between them—Jake says, by the vartue ov his honor, Willie Wales can't be gettin' his money honest."

At this point they had arrived within sight of Clark's abandoned quarry. It was in a dry ravine to the north of the creek bank, where the sections of laminated shales showed out like bands of rust on the face of the rocky wall. As they walked towards it among the broken fragments, Rody began a sage dissertation on the merits of the limestone as a building material. Mr. Thomas soon interrupted him by lifting up a piece of chocolate-colored shale, and demanding:

"Did Mr. Clark ever ship any of this stuff?"

"Is it that ould slate, sir?" said Rody, contemptuously, "no, sir, it's intirely too short and brickle to be good for anythin';—there's some of it in every bluff round here, but we all shovels it wan side whin it comes out wid the good stone."

"Is there much of it of this color?"

"Plinty ov it, sir, black, and brown, an' green, an' crame-colored; it's always in the way of a good blast."

It was now Rody's turn to be surprised and enlightened a little; as Mr. Thomas took the pains to inform him that this was the very kind of rock out of which mineral paint is manufactured. His friend, he intimated, would require an enormous quantity of it, if he found from a few samples that the composition would turn out well.

"I am sorry I have nothing with me to-day," he added, "in which I could carry some specimens for him; and if you will chip me off about twenty pounds of them, I'll take care to have you paid for the trouble, and in a day or two will bring out a valise or something to take them along."

"You needn't talk about payin' for a little sarvice like that, sir," said Rody; "I'll have whips ov them ready for you any time you come out, an' mighty glad to accommodate you, too."

"Thank you, Rody," said the detective, patronizingly, "I'll not forget your civility; and if my friend *does* buy the quarry, I must see about getting you a job to work out the slate for him."

"Long life to you, sir!" said the grateful quarryman, "I knew you wor the raal guinea goold the minute I led me eye on you."

Thomas here observed that it was getting near train-time, and both left the quarry to return towards the bridge. As they were nearing the latter, he turned to his companion, and gazing at him fixedly, said:

"Now, Rody, I suppose you know how to hold your tongue about a matter that concerns yourself. If it is spread abroad that any one wants that quarry stuff for such a use as I have explained, Mr. Clark will raise his price, and my friend won't buy it at all."

"Not a mortial man, sir, 'll know what you're afther

at all, at all—at laste from Rody Maguire," protested that individual with due solemnity.

Another warm punch was the reward of this fealty, and Rody parted from the stranger in the belief that he shared with him an important secret—a belief which, with loyal natures, is the best possible motive for fidelity.

———◆———

CHAPTER IX.

Gossiping to Some Account. —Mayor Wales, of Redrock. —A Slight Mistake in Names.

THE interest which Mr. Thomas had manifested in the mineral resources of Redrock was destined to do further service. It was but feeble progress, indeed, that he could hope to make at Yarmouth, a city eighteen miles distant from the home of Wales. A few of the villagers passed in and out on almost every train, but they were rarely of a class that might serve his purpose; and a mistake of any kind was on no account to be hazarded. A further intercourse with Stanley, the land-agent, must be either unproductive or dangerous; for that gentleman had shown himself such an admirer of the Mayor of Redrock, that any curiosity about the son of that functionary would be sure to attract attention.

In looking over the register at the " Forest "—as loitering hotel guests are wont to do—Thomas discov-

4

ered that W. R. Wales had occasionally made a stay
there; most probably in going to and returning from
the East. But it did not seem quite safe to ask questions of the hotel clerk or servants; for the free-handed
gambler—which he assumed to be the reputation of
Wales—would undoubtedly have entered them on his
lists of friends. Hotel employees, as a class, love the
cheerful giver.

The village itself then, humdrum as it was, and
gossipy and suspicious as are all such humdrum com-
munities, seemed the only good ground for a profitable
research. Even if he must deny himself the luxury of
point-blank questions, he would inevitably learn from
Rody, and without any risk whatever, the cardinal fact
of Wales's return home. The risk of being disemployed
was evidently distressing to the honest quarryman's
mind; and to whom would he reveal the approach of
the blow, if not to the person through whom he expected a new situation?

Accordingly, in a couple of days after his first visit,
the detective again went to Redrock, and walked directly
to the quarry at which Rody was overseer. The day
was wintry and overcast, and a gusty " north-easter "
went sobbing along the creek and in the woods beyond.
The workmen were blue-faced and spiritless, and nib-
bled around their tasks, as if benumbed with the cold, or
as though diligence was out of place in a quarry that
was for sale. The active little foreman alone was

cheery-looking, and showed great satisfaction at again being sought out by the "gintleman from Yarmouth."

"Musha, what med you vinthur out such a cowld day, sir?" was his solicitous greeting to Thomas as the latter came near to him.

"Well, it is rather cold, Rody, but I thought I must look after the box of shales, having since written and promised them to my friend. Did you get me some pieces together, as you promised?"

"I did in throth, sir," was the reply, "an' would have picked you off a whole ton ov thim if you oney gev the word. They're here in the shanty, sure, nice an' snug for you."

"I'm much obliged to you, indeed; I shall take some of them along to-day, anyhow; and I hope they will turn out good for my friend's purpose."

"But what are you goin' to fetch thim in?" advanced the quarryman. "Sure you don't intind to take rocks in your pockets?"

"Oh! not exactly," returned Mr. Thomas; "we must manage it better than that, somehow. I did intend to take out an old valise with me, but I couldn't find one for the purpose. Can't I buy me a little box at the grocer's, and then get it fixed up strong at some smithy around? Or, stay; didn't you tell me there was a tinsmith in the village? Perhaps he might do it."

"Begorra, you're jist right, sir; sure nothing could

be handier than a little box, an' it'll be aisy to get one down the sthreet, an' thin ould Bartlett the tinsmith— it's him I mintioned, sir—could fix it up stout for you to sind an the cars."

"That's the man we want, then; where does he keep shop?"

"It's over in the main sthreet a bit," answered the quarryman; "I think I could show it to you from the brudge yandher."

Whether so designed or not, Mr. Thomas was agreeable enough to take this as a gentle hint, and accepted once more the guidance of Rody. It would have been an easy matter for himself to find both the grocer's and tinsmith's, but he had an obvious purpose to serve in retaining Rody as an adherent at Redrock. In the saloon near the bridge, then, when Bartlett's had been pointed out to him, he again regaled his friend with one of those steaming concoctions that had before won his approval. When this was disposed of, the quarryman himself volunteered to get the box, which he obtained for a few cents, and brought back to Mr. Thomas. Their hot punches being duplicated, the chat was resumed, until the detective carelessly inquired if that man had come along to buy the Anderson quarry yet?

"It's young Wales you're alludin' to," said Rody; "but he isn't to the fore yit; an', indeed—not manin' you an ill answer, sir—it's not much matther if he niver

"You are still afraid, then, that if he takes up the quarry he will appoint a new foreman?"

"Oh! afther all, myself doesn't much mind, sir," said Rody, courageously; "sure I'd get somethin' to live by if the quarries was all undher the say, as I heerd an ould schoolmasther sayin' they wanst was. No, sir; but from what they're beginnin' to say about Willie Wales round here, I don't think the wages that ud come from him ud do a man anney good!"

Thomas didn't think it necessary to controvert this little Hibernianism, and merely rejoined:

"Well, I hope whatever change comes, to see you before long with a more acceptable employer. And now, Rody," he added, "I'll go to the tinsmith's, and if he should fix me this box in good time, I'll bring it to you before taking the train; you can do the packing for me yourself."

"Lave that to me, sir," rejoined Rody; "ayther bring it or sind it, an' I'll cooper up thim slates for you that they'd thravel to Timbuctoo!"

The speaker then turned his face to the creek road, and Mr. Thomas went down the street to carry out his mission at the tinsmith's.

In the rear of an untidy little store, Mr. Jacob Bartlett was found at his work-bench, repairing a wash-boiler for some thrifty village housewife. He readily agreed, for a trifling sum, to furnish with straps, and a pair of hinges, the box which the detective brought with him; and whose purpose he explained, as it were, quite confidentially. The customer being a non-resident, too, he civilly tendered him a chair to await the completion of the job. Thomas, of course, sat down, and passing a cigar to the gratified tinsmith, lit one himself, and proceeded to smoke with quiet complacency.

This Bartlett was a tallish, meager, sallow-faced man, on the shady side of a half century, and in his own village way inclined to be pompous. When the ice was once broken, however, he was an inveterate talker; and proved to be a first-class subject for the inquisitive but cautious detective. He was greatly pleased to hear of the stranger's interest in the product of the quarries, and treated him to an original essay on the resources of all that county, animal, vegetable, and mineral. As the reader may suppose, Mr. Thomas would rather have him talk of its people, having well remembered the observation of Rody Maguire, about his knowledge of, and dislike for, the Wales family. He deemed it most prudent, however, to let the conversation take that turn in a natural way. This it very soon did, through the tinsmith's own curiosity; and when the tide had once set in, Mr. Bartlett revealed himself as a most unsparing character-monger.

It came about thus: While clipping and hammering at the box straps, Jake ventured to inquire of his customer if he had any friends in those parts, when he should decide to work out the slate beds.

"Not a soul," observed Mr. Thomas meekly; "I should be quite a stranger. I did know a family named Wills that left Pennsylvania to locate in the north of Ohio, several years ago; but I can't now remember where it was they settled down."

"I guess them's the very Waleses of Redrock," exclaimed the tinsmith, whose ear had not detected the slight difference of sound; "why, the old chap himself is the Jestice an' Mayor of this here village!"

"It can't be," objected Thomas; "I never thought the man had that much grit in him. He had two or three boys, though, who were lads of much promise."

"They was, eh?" said the tinsmith, dubiously; "wal, I never heern tell rightly whar they come from; but if ever them Wales boys had any promise in 'em, ther's some on 'em gone greatly back on it, that's what *I* know."

"You—don't—say?" suggested Thomas, as if grieved to hear it; but carefully ignoring the tinsmith's mistake on the two names.

This was the old gossip's opportunity, and he fairly reveled in it. He proceeded to assure the stranger that he had no cross grudge against the Wales family, but if the eldest son, Willie, didn't soon change his course, some bad end must come of it. If Willie Wales had ever worked on in a fair business, that people could understand, no one would wonder at him having a few hundred dollars now and again. But so far as the speaker had seen, he was always a rambling idler, and a spendthrift. He ran himself out of several fine situations, and disgraced himself by getting divorced from a good wife, almost before he had a beard. For all that, he could now come into the village every four or five weeks, and swagger around with new clothes, and jewelry, and his pockets stuffed out with bank bills. Heaven only knew how he got them! Jake Bartlett didn't. To be sure, he had boasted to some of the young men, that he won his money at the gambling-tables in New York and Philadelphia; but gamblers didn't win all the time, and that story was too feeble for his, Mr. Bartlett's, credulity.

Thus far into the ruins of Willie Wales's reputation had Jake proceeded, almost without question or interruption from his customer. Mr. Thomas, indeed, was greatly charmed with the volubility of the tinsmith; and by a few gentle ejaculations, carelessly thrown in, now managed to learn that this doubtful character was the eldest of three brothers, of whom the youngest, a lively youth, was a telegraph operator at the depot. Willie himself had been home for a short time only two weeks before, and had then exhibited a roll of about six hundred dollars in bank notes, to some admiring companions, in the hotel near the station.

The detective further gleaned that Wales, the father,

had once obstructed Jake Bartlett in his aspirations for some village office, and in this he seemed to perceive the animus of the tinsmith.

"Thar goes the old cuss now," exclaimed Bartlett, as he looked out from his store into the village street; "an' he carries it right slick on his jedgeship and his mayorship."

Thomas looked out too, and looked intently, that he might be able to recognize the head of the family that was becoming so interesting to him. A silver-haired, ruddy-faced, prosperous-looking gentleman, it may be stated, appeared to the observer Mayor Wales of Redrock.

"Oh! that's not the *Wills* I knew," exclaimed the detective, as he turned to Jake: "the Pennsylvania Wills was at least four inches taller, and sharp as a fence-post."

"But it ain't Wills," retorted Jake, "it's Wales I'm a talkin' about all the time. That was Jedge Wales, Mayor of Redrock."

"Not the same family at all," repeated Thomas; "and, besides, I know that the eldest son was a good, moral young fellow."

"Wal, there ain't no much moral about our Waleses, either root or branch. Why, the old deacon himself goes around among the women folks here, as if he was a young buck of thirty."

This branch of the subject had no interest for

4*

Thomas, however, and the box being now completed, he arranged with Jake to have it sent to Rody Maguire, who was to pack it and care for it till the owner's next visit. Mr. Thomas then left, but made a point to loiter at the express office over some needed information as to the shipment of his box of specimens. His main purpose, however, was to get a good view of Wales, the telegraph operator, which he eventually did; but ascertained at the same time that he was the night operator, and only came occasionally in the day-time to oblige his telegraphic colleague.

CHAPTER X.

A Flood of New Light.—More Forgeries.—How the Caution of H. B. Claflin, the noted New York Merchant, Preserved the Express Company from another Depredation.—Interesting Intelligence from Pittsburg.—The Jealousy of Government Bureaus.

WHILE our emissary was thus scouting from his ambush at Yarmouth, a flood of new light was pouring in at the Philadelphia agency. Through the well-directed inquiries of Mr. Bangs we were soon placed in possession, not only of the most essential details of the felonies already known, but of advices concerning others which presaged even a bolder and deeper criminality on the part of the men in whose pursuit we had engaged.

As my son Robert continued his researches at the headquarters of the various express companies, he was enabled to furnish Mr. Bangs with the particulars of the forgery at Rochester on the United States Express Company. The draft made use of was for $770, and had been drawn on a New York bank by the Commercial National Bank of Oshkosh, Wis., payable to the order of a certain Samuel Little, of Boston. Mr. Little never received the letter in which this draft was mailed, and the collection of the amount was effected by a man who styled himself R. W. Davis, engaged for an interval in the lumber trade at Rochester. The signature of this Davis gave every indication of having been written by the self-same penman who was Dudley, Randall, and Cone by turns.

But there were still other cases, and the trail of the same serpent was over them all. It was stated that in the early part of the winter an attempt had been made at Albany, New York, to collect simultaneously three drafts through the agency of the American Merchants' Union Express. These instruments also were from western sources, and aggregated a total of more than two thousand dollars, which was duly remitted to Albany for account of the presentor, a Mr. C. H. Rugby. Happily, the express agent in that city was particularly scrupulous in the matter of identification, or else the forger was remiss in his preparations therefor, and the money was refused to him and sent back to New York.

As it subsequently transpired, the daring swindler had promptly followed; and learning at the company's central office that the money was to hand, professed his pleasure thereat, and promised to obtain a more satisfactory identification in the metropolis itself. On arrival he had registered at one of the leading hotels, and thence he sallied forth next day to the warehouse of H. B. Claflin & Co., prominent wholesale dealers in dry goods. To the senior of that firm he now presented a letter purporting to come from a customer in Kansas City, Mo., and introducing the bearer, Mr. C. H. Rugby of the same place, as an intending purchaser. Mr Rugby, said the letter, was about to open a new store, and as a reputable and rising young merchant, was recommended to the kindly attention of the great wholesalers.

In a natty little speech Mr. Rugby himself stated that he must defer his selection of goods till the afternoon and morrow, as his funds were still lying at the office of the Express Company, through which he had for safety remitted them.

"I have already indorsed my drafts, Mr. Claflin," added the plausible Mr. Rugby, "and if you will send one of your representives with me to the express office, to identify me, I can draw the amounts, and then we proceed to business."

"Certainly, my dear sir," was the reply of the merchant, as he looked once more from his visitor to the open letter; "we always like to accommodate our western friends. I shall just drop a telegram—*pro forma*, you know,—to Smith & Co., of Kansas City, to see that their introduction is all right, and as we shall have an answer in an hour or two, you will have plenty of time to realize your funds, and select your stock."

"I shall call in then, I suppose, about one o'clock, sir," was the question of the now uneasy forger.

"Say two—two o'clock, Mr. Rugby," answered the cautious old merchant, "we are sure to have a telegram by that time."

Mr. Rugby looked thankful, and went out humming a tune—but entirely forgot to return again. In due course the telegram was answered from Kansas City, Messrs. Smith & Co. repudiating the letter of introduction.

From the facts just narrated, and the general accordance of penmanship and descriptions, Mr. Bangs was strengthened in his first impression that the forgeries had all been perpetrated by one adroit swindler; while the boldness of his movements in connection with those Albany drafts indicated a man of consummate nerve and fertility of resources.

From Pittsburg, Pa., where our swindler had been known as Robert L. Dudley, now came also the first few facts of a definite personal bearing. They were contained in a response from Mr. Srively to the renewed application of Mr. Bangs for all particulars that could be gleaned of the forger. From these it appeared that Dudley had been some time a resident of Pittsburg, and married, while there, a Miss Greenleaf of Alleghany City, a flourishing suburb of the first-named place. A sister of the same Miss Greenleaf, with her husband, Dr. Marsh, were still residents; and Dudley and wife used frequently to dine with them after the marriage of the latter. The forger was last engaged in the preparation of a city directory—being pretty well known as its intending publisher—and found no difficulty whatever in collecting the La Crosse draft. Immediately thereafter, both himself and wife were missing from Pittsburg. To this information Mr. Snively appended a more minute description of Dudley, which had been revised by a Mr. Loomis, an insurance agent, to whom the "directory man" was personally well known.

Once more Mr. Bangs was struck by the general conformity with the descriptions of Cone and Randall. Nor did the superintendent fail to make a note of the Greenleaf family, as a possible clue to the whereabouts of Dudley, if the trail at Redrock should prove to be ineffectual.

But the intercourse of the superintendent with the post-office authorities at Washington was that which brought about the most agreeable results of all. His first proceeding, as determined, had been to communicate the outlines of the forgery cases to Mr. J. L.

McPhail, of the department of Special Service, and to inform him of the part we had undertaken in regard to the forgers. The idea of co-operative action was most delicately broached, but accompanied with such arguments as to its value in the parallel investigations, as had seemed most convincing to his own logical mind. He conceived that these must impress the official dragon that co-operation with us would best subserve even its own designs; and that for once it would be well, in the very interests of justice, to set aside the traditional jealousy with which government bureaus regard the intervention of outsiders.

Nor was he mistaken. On the receipt of this strong communication, Mr. McPhail held a conference at the national capital with S. B. Cochran, Esq., Chief of the Bureau of Mail Depredations. As a result, he was authorized to inform Mr. Bangs that an investigation into the loss of some of these very drafts had been instituted some time before by Mr. J. S. Elwell, Special Agent of the Post-Office at Chicago.

A very gracious letter of introduction to this Mr. Elwell was also forwarded, in which the conviction of Mr. Cochran was expressed, that Elwell would find it profitable to act with Mr. Pinkerton. This was only given as an opinion, however, and was not accompanied by any instructions from the chief to his subordinate. The letter was at once transmitted to me at Chicago, and to Mr. Frank Warner, my superintendent at headquarters, was entrusted the delicate mission of using it to good purpose. The measure of success which this gentleman achieved was at once creditable to his diplomacy, and most valuable to our operation; but here it will be more in order to relate by what outside methods of detection Mr. Bangs was leading us to the very same platform.

CHAPTER XI.

A Revelation.—Further Conferences with the Postal Authorities.

ONE of the first ideas of the Superintendent, after arranging his programme in Philadelphia, was to anticipate as far as possible a refusal of information from bureaucratic sources. With this view he had written to Governor Washburn at La Crosse, and to the other makers and first holders of the drafts, to inquire the exact day and hour on which the letters containing them had been mailed, and the address of the parties in the East to whom they had been sent.

These details were furnished him as to four of the drafts, of which one was that known to have been forged by Cone. Now, taking into account the origin and destination of the several letters, Mr. Bangs could at once determine that they must have been stolen either at the post-office at Toledo, or at some point to the east of that city; for they had all originated in Toledo it-

self, or would take through it an easterly route by the
Lake Shore and Michigan Southern Railroad. But the
very fact that they had *not* all originated at Toledo, but
one or two at points further eastward, indicated almost
beyond doubt that they were purloined *while in transit.*
This pointed the superintendent's suspicions, as a matter
of course, to the postal agents and transmitting clerks
on the route just named.

But this field of investigation was further narrowed
down by the facts pertaining to one of the Cone drafts.

This instrument, which was put in for collection at
Philadelphia, Pa., on January 9th, was now ascertained
to have been mailed at Toledo on January the 7th, just
forty-eight hours before. Had it gone the entire way
to Boston, its proper destination, it were easy to see that
it could not have been remailed there, or even carried
by the forger, and reach Philadelphia within the period
named. Hence came the conclusion that the letters
must have been stolen between Toledo and Albany, a
which latter city the mails for New England diverged
from the main route.

But further yet: Supposing the forger to have
started south from Albany, the margin of time left to
reach Philadelphia, and manipulate the forgery, would
still be inadequate. The assumption became inevitable
that the draft left the Lake Shore mail route at a point
further west, most probably at Cleveland or Erie, from

both of which cities there were lines direct through Pennsylvania.

"These letters have been stolen from the mail cars between Toledo and Erie," had now become the verdict of the incisive superintendent.

Planting himself on this theory, Mr. Bangs made a polite application to the department at Washington, to be furnished with the lists of mail clerks who did duty on the cars of that route on the four dates he had selected. Through the good offices of Mr. Cochran, four lists, corresponding with the four dates, were forwarded to him, each containing the names of four postal clerks, which was the quota detailed for that special duty.

Now, here was a revelation. Out of the total of sixteen names, twelve were of different clerks, neither of whom chanced in any two of the details. A thirteenth name, on the contrary, was present in all four of them! It was that of one James Hobart.

That this postal clerk was with the mails, on duty, on each occasion when one of those draft letters was stolen, was, to say the least of it, a very singular coincidence. Mr. Bangs, indeed, was of opinion that he ought to be kept in sight; and so advised me when communicating to headquarters his methods and his deductions.

I return, then, once more to the "Great Northwest." When Mr. Warner, armed with the letter of

introduction from Washington, presented himself at
Chicago to Special Agent Elwell, he found that gentleman to be both practical and accommodating; with perfect good grace he acknowledged the value of the
co-operation suggested by his chief, and admitted that
for several months past he had been on the look-out in
his district for the thief who purloined the earlier of
those draft letters.

The movements of one man, in particular, he said,
had been closely watched, and so many suspicious circumstances attached to him, that he felt morally certain of his guilt. One of these was, for instance, that
he had come out of his mail car one night on the platform at Cleveland, having just put a bunch of letters
in his pocket, and there stood waiting for a while as if
some one had appointed to meet him. No person appearing, he returned to his car just as the train started;
and furtively, as it was reported, threw back the letters
into a side-box.

"But a moral certainty of his guilt," concluded Mr.
Elwell, "will not amount to a legal conviction; and the
evidence yet to hand is quite insufficient thereto. It is
true that a sudden arrest might force out some fresh
proofs; but that is a very extreme measure, and one I
should not care to undertake unless the result were
more certain."

Mr. Warner here proceeded to review the facts concerning those early drafts already known to our

Agency. At the mention of Dudley's name, Elwell interrupted by the statement that he knew all about that party, and had labored hard for his capture as an accomplice of the mail thief. In so doing he had acquainted himself with the antecedents of Dudley at Pittsburg, and followed him up quite closely after he fled from that city. The clever forger had always eluded his grasp, however, and he believed he was now somewhere in Michigan going under the name of R. K. Livingstone.

"I know it is he," added the special agent, "from the description that has been given me; although my last informant stated that the fellow's whiskers were only of two or three weeks' growth—probably, he cut them off and is letting them grow again. However," he concluded with emphasis, "if I could only catch that scoundrel I might rake in the mail thief without any hesitation!"

Without specifying full particulars, Mr. Warner now convinced the official that my Agency had a most promising clue on Dudley, and had good grounds to hope for his speedy capture.

At this Elwell expressed his great satisfaction, and gratified my superintendent with the assurance that he would give us all possible help and information consistent with his obligations to the department. He would like to be on hand, too, he said, whenever we had arranged to seize on the forger, as he thought it would

also be the right moment to pounce on the guilty mail
clerk.

In reply, Mr. Warner intimated that it was not
our purpose to startle either of the criminals by pre-
cipitate action, but to hold our clue patiently in hand
until the movements of one would reveal the others.
For this reason it was important that we should know
any other persons who were suspected, as the contact of
our man with them would then become intelligible.

On this Mr. Elwell made no further hesitation in
stating that the object of his suspicions was one James
Hobart, a clerk on the Eastern mail route ; and that he
had been already docked for dismissal from the service,
but was retained at his duty for the purposes of this
investigation.

This closed the interview, but the information obtained, and the kindly disposition of the post-office
people to work with us, seemed to add to our assurances
of final success. My readers will desire, then, to again
visit Redrock, which had already become to us the key
of the position.

CHAPTER XII.

The Return of Wales.— The Geological Thomas also on Land.

THE return of Wales to the paternal roof at Redrock at last came about. It was on a day when
the geological Mr. Thomas had also gone to the village,
on an anxious mission for additional slate specimens.
The box of these treasures—which he claimed to have
dispatched to his mythical friend—had strayed away by
some villainous express route. What, then, could be
more natural than to deplore its loss with the sympathetic Rody, and engage him to prepare a fresh supply ?
This was quite easily arranged; a good warm punch or
two, and the unwonted luxury of a cigar, being thought
ample return by the quarryman for the trifling labor it
involved. The provision of another packing-box was
also discussed between them, and arranged for, and then
countermanded, with such artful indecision, as to leave
fairly open to the detective an excuse for further nego-
tiations. Neither Rody nor Jake Bartlett, indeed, to
whom Thomas also paid a visit, could make out entirely
to his own satisfaction whether the gentleman was
seriously anxious to have those specimens hastened forward or not.

Nor was it the design of Mr. Thomas that they
should be. Danger from either of these worthies, per-

haps, was not to be apprehended; but the stake at issue was far too great to be left to the hazard of even a rustic's penetration. The flight or escape of Wales, through any indiscretion on his own part, our detective would have looked upon as an irretrievable disgrace.

In the course of the afternoon the officer had returned to the railroad depot, and managed to engage in conversation about his missing box with the dapper little express agent. While the chat was in progress, young Wales, the telegraph operator, walked in from the instrument room, and cheerily exclaimed to his neighbor—

"Tom, I've just got a dispatch from our Willie; he's coming up on the 'Eight-forty'!"

The expressman nodded his congratulations, and the youth hastened into the village, with the open telegram in his hand; no doubt to exhibit its contents to the other members of the family.

Mr. Thomas didn't loiter much longer at the vicinity of the depot. He needed to moderate his eager expectancy, and to await in tranquillity the momentous "Eight-forty." The human quarry in whose pursuit he had set forth was now almost at hand; and like huntsmen after meaner game, he had all the febrile enthusiasm of the chase. In a secluded place, he took from his pocket my most recent telegram, and carefully reperused its pithy instructions:

"Use additional caution at Redrock. Telegraph in·
stantly Wales's arrival. Get good spot on him, and
then shadow from Yarmouth with untiring vigilance.
Note well his associates and movements, especially on
arrival and departure of trains.

"ALLAN PINKERTON."

"Oh! yes, I'll shadow him," soliloquized Mr.
Thomas; "his own finger-nails never stuck as close to
him as I will to this *very successful gambler!*"

Neither W. R. Wales nor any of his welcoming
friends took notice that evening of the quiet young
man who was amongst them on the platform of the
railroad depot at Redrock. He was a person, indeed,
who was decidedly with them, though not of them.
He whistled meditatively, or hummed spasmodically, as
he glanced down with interest at his spattered boots, or
anxiously along the line, like one waiting for the down-
train. Whilst they hustled and mingled, exchanging
their boisterous greetings, he meandered around them
in this self-abstracted way; always near to them, yet
always as if moving away from them; constantly observing, while seeming unobservant. And here is what
this very preoccupied young man, Mr. Thomas, managed
to note on that interesting occasion:

When the Eight-forty train from Yarmouth slowed
up at the depot, the usual five or six Redrock passengers stepped from the cars, and slowly sauntered into

the light near the entry door—as persons who, having reached near home, are no longer in any disposition to haste. Of these five or six persons, one was a young man of far less rustic appearance than any of his fellow-passengers. Indeed he might be called a stylish young man, and classed with those that adorn—as they often defile—the promenades of our great cities. Rather taller than the medium five feet eight, he was slender in build, and looked about thirty years of age. His features were pale, and delicate of outline, and a yellowish mustache drooped around his mouth. The whiskers were of the same sandy tinge, but were only of about three weeks' growth, and were cut short from about the middle of the jaw with mathematical precision. His hair was of a blackish brown, and showed a marked contrast with the color of his whiskers, as if chemicals had lent darkness to its natural hue.

The dress of this individual was in the prevailing fashion, both as to cut and finish; and he wore the high silk hat so infrequent on rustic polls—all alike being evidently new. He also wore, or rather sported, a quantity of jewelry; of which Thomas could discern, even in the gloom, a diamond finger ring and breast-pin, and a very showy gold watch-guard. In his hand he carried a newish-looking valise, and over one arm a comfortable traveling wrap.

As this well-appointed personage crossed the platform, there stepped forth to greet him—from a group

5

near the waiting room door,—young Wales the telegraph clerk. After the uncouth manner of his age and
kind, he extended his hand to the traveler and made
the somewhat needless inquiry :

"Hallo ! Will; did you get up ?"

"Yes; just as you see," was the curt response of
his migratory brother—for this shining traveler was
W. R. Wales.

The Mayor of Redrock was also close by, and next
shook hands with his hopeful son. He then exchanged
with him a few undertoned remarks, and taking the
valise and wrap into his charge, turned out into the
street, as if to spare him to the courtesies of the younger
men of the group.

In the midst of the latter Willie Wales was soon
standing, with hat lifted, and running his fingers fop-
pishly through his hair—the target for a cross-fire of
noisy questions. When not quite meaningless, these
were of that stereotyped inanity with which young
men of the period greet a returned excursionist :—"Did
you have good fun, Will?" "Stop any at Yarmouth
coming up?" "Did you make a run into New York
this time ?" "Have a good time East, Willie ?" "Say,
Wales, how was *biz* with you this time ?"

The reply to this last question alone was of any
great interest to Thomas; and luckily he was in a position both to hear and see.

"Tip-top, sonny !" were the words used by Wales,

who at the same time slapped his hand gayly over his breast pocket; as if the proof were reposing in the billbook which it sheltered.

One of the young men—who were all, evidently, "hail fellows well met" with Wales—now presumed to extract from his pocket the gold watch which it contained. Holding it up tenderly and admiringly in the light, he exclaimed:

"By gum!—new ticker this trip, Will?"

"Yes, sirree!" responded Wales, "I bought her down to New York, in one of the nobbiest stores."

"I reckon *she* cost a little pile?" pursued the inspector of the timepiece, with almost painful interest.

"You just bet, Charlie," answered its proprietor, with a smirk of almost girlish vanity; "just two hundred and fifty dollars, every dime of it."

One and another of the coterie then took the watch to examine it in turn, and bestow on it an admiring ejaculation; when at last it came to an individual who possibly saw clearer than the rest.

"Why, Will," he remarked, "she's an hour ahead of time!"

"Oh!—thunder!" explained Wales, "that's New York time; give her to me."

In a confused and pettish manner, he now restored the watch to his pocket.

"But come, boys!" he exclaimed in a moment

after; "let us go over to old Kramer's and have a smile of his cognac. I'm pretty well used up after the ride, and want to get home and have a good snooze."

The entire party then shuffled into the street, and across to the depot hotel. The detective had ensconced himself near the door of the waiting-room, where he could get one more comprehensive view of Wales. This being accomplished, he dropped back into the friendly darkness; but could see through Kramer's oft-opened door that other villagers were not loth to take the hand of their disreputable neighbor—in tribute, no doubt, to his readiness to "stand treat." Mr. Thomas was now satisfied. His game was safely and unsuspectingly housed, and for the present, at least, he had no further business at Redrock.

He returned by the next train to Yarmouth, telegraphed me in cipher of the arrival of Wales, and then wrote out the mail reports that covered this day's doings.

--------•--------

CHAPTER XIII.

That Packing-Box again.—Cynical Jake Bartlett, and what is Disclosed by his Chatter.— Working in the Right Track.

THE arrival of Wales at his home had made the ambush of Detective Thomas a delicate matter. The great importance of not alarming him had been

sufficiently impressed upon him, but it was equally in-
cumbent on him to obtain information about his movements. The manner, therefore, in which Wales would
deport himself among his Redrock neighbors became a
subject of special anxiety to the officer. That he was
a shrewd and daring criminal there was now every
warrant for believing; but had not the proof transpired
that he was also a boastful and conceited fop?

What was more likely, then, that in this latter
character he would deeply betray himself at the village? And how was the Agency to learn of his im-
prudences? Who was to take advantage of his self-
criminations? These were reflections that distressed
Operative Thomas exceedingly, constrained as he was
by prudential reasons to keep aloof from Redrock, and
privileged to do little more than watch the railroad
which was its eastern outlet.

" He is among his friends now," the detective would
reflect; "and he would go swaggering and lionizing
around that blessed village, with not a shadow to take
care of him, and not a creature to know when he gives
himself away! Too bad! too bad!"

In his professional anguish, Detective Thomas received some comfort from a telegram which I now sent
him from Chicago. It was to the effect that my home
superintendent, Mr. Warner, would soon join him at
Yarmouth; that a warrant for the arrest of Wales was
in contemplation; and that parties would be sent from

the East to identify him. In the Agency at this time the impression was somewhat general that he must be Randall; while, from a comparison with the descriptions he had obtained, Thomas had decided for himself that he was Dudley. I have already commented, however, on the fallibility of personal descriptions, particularly those from an unprofessional source.

The third morning from the return of Wales, Mr. Thomas sauntered into the depot at Yarmouth, when whom should he see stepping off the Redrock train but that individual himself! The fact was, that the detective was constantly on the watch for such an event; but to look at him just then, one would suppose he had no other object in life than to recover a stray trunk—so intent was he in examining a pile of those articles that stood near the baggage-office.

No sooner, however, had Wales passed from the depot into the street, than his shadow was there too. And whither, for a time, the forger bent his footsteps, thither also went his unrecognized shadow. In a few of the more crowded thoroughfares there was but little difficulty in keeping Wales in view. But it was observable that the rogue was ill at ease. Every new and then he stopped in his way, like a person in deep thought, and furtively glanced around as though to learn if he were followed. After a while, too, with the cunning of an old pickpocket. he turned into a region of quiet streets, where it would be difficult to hold him

in sight for many successive blocks without the detective being himself detected.   He was manifestly in that
stage of conscious guilt, that

> "Fills the light air with visionary terrors,
>   And shapeless forms of fear."

Thomas saw how it was with him, and then made
up his mind.   He was not the kind of officer to go
dodging around street corners at a risk, when logic
would bear him in security to the issue.   Wales, he
concluded, was not going away, anyhow.   He had evidently come to Yarmouth for a little tour of business—
or of pleasure, mayhap, if the riotings of the vicious
can be called by that name.   He was dressed much
more quietly than on his late brilliant descent into Redrock ; and he had neither parcel nor traveling equipment
of any kind along with him.   No ; certainly Wales was
not going away.

And so the shadow decided to withdraw himself,
and pick up his man again on the return to the depot.

In due course of time this self-denial was rewarded.
Towards five o'clock in the afternoon, while on a vigi-
lant outlook from the entry hall of the Forest Hotel,
Thomas descried Wales returning in the direction of
the station.   A train, he was aware, would leave for
Redrock a few minutes after five.

An idea flashed upon the detective.   Wales was
going home for the night—now, wasn't this the very

chance to get the news at the village ? It might be too late to see Rody, for he would be resting after his day's labor in his humble home. But there was the invaluable Jake Bartlett—babbler by instinct, and self-elected censor of the morals and methods of the Wales family. Why, Jake would by this time be bubbling over with scandal !

Thomas though nct another moment ; or, if he did, thought only, that in detective as in other difficulties, the man who hesitates is lost. He hurried to the depot, saw Wales into a car, took a seat in the next coach behind, and in an hour thereafter had fluttered through the Redrock depot, like the shadow that he was, and was rapidly striding up the back road to the head of the village. An appetizing luxury, indeed, it would have been to Mr. Thomas, to remain near Wales when they descended at the depot, and shadow his movements in the lower part of Redrock. But the hotel and two or three stores that were near the depot made that vicinity a sort of thoroughfare ; and the risk of being remarked was proportionately great. For the present, therefore, he must be content with second-hand information.

Walking around the creek road the detective came down from the bridge, and entered Jake Bartlett's dingy establishment. The tinsmith had ceased work for the day, and was seated on a stove in his shop, chatting with two villagers similarly disposed. With an air of business urgency Thomas saluted him, and inquired about "that other packing-box;" adding that his friend had become so very impatient in the matter that he was induced to come down that evening to see to it.

The astonished Mr. Bartlett reminded him that he had left no definite order; and that though he had indeed spoken of a packing-box, he said not a word about when it was required.

With a feint of self-reproach Mr. Thomas had to admit that this was so; and then asked Jake if he would not make up a small one on the morrow, and have it sent to Rody the quarryman, who knew what further was to be done. It being a case of prepayment the tinsmith readily promised; and, the business matter being settled, invited his customer to a seat, as the latter must wait more than an hour for the next train to Yarmouth.

The detective wished for nothing better; and having sat down, produced his trusty cigar-case, from which he regaled all three of the villagers with a weed. Smoking, he well knew, promotes, rather than obstructs, the flow of masculine gossip.

"How are times, Mr. Bartlett?" he inquired after a short silence—being assured from the looks of the villagers that they regarded his presence purely in a business aspect.

"Wal, ther ain't nothin' pertikler to boast on, Mister; but we was jest a sayin' that it *is* curious how

5*

some folks kin git along, an' hev piles of money, an' never do nothin' fur it—while them as is honest, an' works hard, kin skeerce grub out a livin'."

The detective at once perceived that the talk was just where he wanted it, so he made the cheerful and natural inquiry :

"How now ?—has somebody been finding a gold mine round here ?"

"It looks putty much that way," answered the tin-smith, " on'y it's a kind o' goold mine thet on'y one can dig into—leastways ther's on'y one seems to know whar 'tis. It's thet young fellar, the Jedge's son, that I spoke to you about, Mister—he on'y went East here two or three weeks ago, an' he's to hum now, an' not less than seven or eight thousen dollar in his pocket. See now, sir ?"

"But it's ten thousen he hes, Jake," interposed one of the villagers; "I heern tell thet he showed over nine thousen in bills to young Georgie Striker !"

"Guess you're both on you rayther wide o' the mark," said villager number two; "Frank Johnson oughter know, for he hed a drink of him at the depot, night he come up, an' he says Willie Wales hes got every picayune of fifteen thousen dollars !"

"Howsumdever," said Mr. Bartlett, authoritatively, "ther' ain't no doubt but what he brought five thousen dollars to the city this mornin'. Farmer Granger is a man as wouldn't tell no lie about it, an' he seed him

put that much in the First National at Yarmouth, when
he was cashin' a check fur his *pro*juice."

"This gold-finder of yours is a gentleman who
takes good care of his money, then?" pleasantly suggested Mr. Thomas.

"He takes keer of it for his *own*, Mister;" said the
tinsmith, bitterly, "an' fur hisself—that's about all.
Folks say as how he gev the old Jedge five hundred
dollar fur a gift, an' a goold watch an' chain to one
brother, an, an—it's all in the family anyhow—whatever it is they're all in the same kittle. Faro bank, indeed!—*he* make all that money in a faro bank! No,
sir; he can't come that story in Redrock."

"But I hear he's done gamblin'," again struck in
one of the gossips; "thet he's goin' to buy the quarry
this time sure, an' go to church, an' settle down for a
steady life."

"Mebbe he will, an' mebbe he won't," said the
cynical Jake Bartlett;—"but if it's an honest trade he
hes now he might as well stick to it;—there ain't many
honest ways of makin' five thousan' dollar a week."

Without appearing to take part in this conversation,
or even to be much interested by it, Mr. Thomas
spurred it along gently until he had learned about all
that the villagers had to tell. His anticipations about
how Wales would demean himself were fully borne
out by what he now learned. Since his arrival at Redrock, the swindler had careered round the village like a

person crazed with unwonted riches; exhibiting to all who would admire his diamonds, and his watch, and ostentatiously opening his plunder-filled wallet on every imaginable pretext. Although temperate as to ardent spirits, too, his inordinate vanity had made him garrulous as a drunkard in his cups. To one he had spoken of his faro bank in Philadelphia; to another he had boasted that "there was more where that came from,"—alluding to his money; and several heard him make reference to his "partner in the East."

On this last point one villager had now recalled, that shortly before his last trip from home, Wales showed him a telegram, which he claimed to be from this partner, and which said : "Come week after next, the market will then be better." Neither the name of the partner, however, nor the city from whence he telegraphed, were noticed by the bumpkin.

Mr. Thomas was quite crammed with such fragments of gossip as these, when he reached Yarmouth, late that night. It was in "the wee sma' hours ayont the twal" that he succeeded in framing them into a connected report. To the Agency—need it be stated? —they brought fresh assurance that we were working in the right track.

CHAPTER XIV.

Another Move with an Unsuccessful Result.—The Problem of Identification as far as ever from Solution.—A newly-discovered Jewel of Intelligence.

PLEASANT as it was to be convinced that we had struck the right trail, it was no easy matter to determine at this point what our action should be. This nine days' wonder that was mystifying the villagers of Redrock was also, it must be admitted, a source of much perplexity to the Agency. The great problem of the moment was—who was this man Wales?

I was certain that he was just the man we wanted; but that was not enough. What was his *alias*, and which his crimes? The information and reports which continued to reach us, digested as they were with anxious care, were making it hourly more questionable whether he would fit any of the forgery cases. And if not, would not his arrest be one of those blunders that are said to be worse than crimes?

The description of Wales furnished to us by Thomas agreed tolerably well with those we had obtained of Cone. But Cone had sent a letter to Wales; and men do not ordinarily take the trouble to write to themselves. This would imply a case of dual consciousness only to be found in the realms of lunacy.

And how could this Wales be Dudley? Had we not obtained from Mr. Snively, of Pittsburg, confirmed through Special Agent Elwell, a record of Dudley and his career that was circumstantial even to the particulars of his marriage? The conjugal history of Wales, was also now known to us, and embraced such different facts as could only pertain to a distinct individual.

Next came the likelihood that Wales might be the person who had called himself Randall—or he might be Davis, or Rugby—for all their descriptions bore the same general outline. But here under our eyes were the signatures made by these various forgers, and they were completely identical with the streaky, long-backed scrawl from Dudley's pen—while to crown the difficulty, the writing of Wales himself, of which Thomas sent specimens from the Forest Hotel, showed no resemblance whatever to that used in any of the forgeries!

Not being in the postal service, he was certainly not the mail-clerk Hobart, whom Elwell suspected, and Bangs had theorized into criminal existence. Hobart, indeed, we now knew personally.

None of all these, apparently, was Wales of Redrock, and yet I felt convinced he was the very man we wanted!

In this dilemma, the General Superintendent, Mr. Linden, and myself, met together by telegraphic appointment in Philadelphia, to hold conference with

Mr. Coleman of the Adams Express Company on the subject of identification. I urged on this gentleman the advisability of sending on to Yarmouth the Newark express officer who had known the forger Randall. Mr. Thomas could readily point out to him the person of W. R. Wales, and once for all it could be determined if he were the perpetrator of the Newark swindle.

The express agent in question was an intelligent young man named Alonzo Wilson, and being communicated with by telegraph, expressed his readiness— though suffering from ill health—to leave Newark for Yarmouth that very evening, and report to Mr. Thomas at the Forest Hotel.

And right here, where events at all points of our operation crowd each other closely, I propose to take my readers directly along with him, that the result of his mission may be the sooner known. Let me prepare them for the journey, however, by stating, that to anticipate the expected identification, I now caused Mr. Linden to procure a United States warrant of arrest, charging—with all customary verbiage—that W. R. Wales, otherwise called R. L. Dudley, R. D. Randall, R. W. Davis, T. H. Cone, and R. K. Livingstone, did on or about the 1st of January, "steal, take, and carry away from the United States mail a certain letter or package certaining a draft or order for the payment of money." This warrant, which was accompanied by the necessary affidavits, was comprehensive enough to meet every aspect of the case, the acts of any of the forgers being only made possible by the prior crimes of theft.

To give it effect in the Ohio district, the instrument was sent for indorsement to my old friend Judge Sherman of Cleveland, who was also to appoint Thomas a United States deputy marshal to assist in its execution. I next instructed my Chicago Superintendent, Mr. Warner, to obtain the documents in Cleveland, and proceed with them in person to Yarmouth, there to give counsel to Thomas when all was ripe for the arrest of Wales.

We may now alight at the Forest Hotel and rejoin the impatient detective. By this time Wales had apparently lulled himself into security, and was in the habit of coming into the city almost every day. Mr. Thomas was thus spared considerable uneasiness, and saved from the perils of hovering around Redrock. In Yarmouth, however, he shadowed his man most assiduously. The visits of Wales were now principally to the bank, and other places of business. Thomas found no difficulty, therefore, in learning that he had now, at last, purchased the quarry, and was proceeding to work it as if he had indeed settled down—to grow respectable, as it were, on his crime-earned capital. The very material knowledge of what checks he drew, and to whom payable, was readily furnished by the bank—for all reputable business concerns are found willing to assist my officers, knowing them to be legitimate instruments of justice.

In the railroad freight-shed, too, Mr. Thomas had inspected several lots of implements for the quarry, and from the way they were addressed, found that the second brother of the swindler had been placed in charge. He also had the humanity to inquire, and the charity to rejoice at, the news that Rody Maguire had been kept on as the working foreman—a fact which is here noted to disprove the claim of the unthinking, that detectives are a hard, unfeeling class of men. There be many of the profession that I know of, whose charities, indeed, might shine as the stars.

Mr. Thomas easily recognized Alonzo Wilson, on his arrival at the hotel, and assisted him to select comfortable quarters—the young man being much cut up by his illness, and the fatigues of the long railroad journey. It was three days afterwards before he was able to be about, or that the detective found a chance to point out Wales to him. This befell at the railroad depot, as the swindler stepped down one morning from the Redrock train.

Together they then followed him through the principal streets, occasionally catching glimpses of his side face as he moved along through the streams of pedestrians. The detective looked from time to time into the countenance of his companion—still quite blanched from recent sickness—but saw there no signs of the desired recognition. All was a pallid, unpromising blank.

"Well?" he muttered at last, after an unusually good chance had presented itself for examining the face of Wales. The latter had stopped full in their way on a street corner, and turned fairly round to speak with a man who met and greeted him.

"Well, now?" repeated the detective, after they had sauntered past Wales, and were safe beyond his hearing.

"That's not Randall," said the young expressman, who with knitted brow was moving his head negatively from side to side.

"Sure of that?"

"Perfectly," was the emphatic reply; "that's not the fellow who collected the drafts at Newark."

With this discouraging report, they retraced their steps to the Forest, where Mr. Warner, who was now in Yarmouth, awaited their return anxiously. The Superintendent advised another good inspection before Wales should go back to Redrock. The opportunity for this occurred during the afternoon, when the object of their attentions chanced right into the reading-room of the Forest. But the result this time was no different—according to young Wilson, at least, W. R. Wales and R. D. Randall were not the same individual.

"So much decided, perhaps," remarked Mr. Warner quietly, as he made his preparations to return to Chicago, to assist in the concert of fresh measures. Before quitting Yarmouth, however, he instructed Thomas to unabated vigilance over the movements of Wales. He also made arrangements for the stay of the young man Wilson for four or five days more. After a more ample rest—he hoped—and complete restoration to his normal physical condition, he might yet recognize in Wales the forger Randall. A considerable time had elapsed since Wilson saw the latter, and the Superintendent well knew that the faculty of memory may be greatly disturbed by the alternations of bodily strength. That which, of sound or form, is best remembered in health, is frequently distorted or effaced from the mind in illness; while the long-forgotten melodies and faces of childhood will often be vividly perceptible to the senses of the sick.

Besides, there was still the chance that Wales might be visited at Yarmouth by some one or other of his associates in crime, and in this way might Randall be discovered to Mr. Wilson, if not in the person of Wales himself.

The possibility that Wales might be Dudley, had now at once to be disposed of. Through the medium of the Express Company, therefore, I procured to be sent from Pittsburg the Mr. Loomis who had known Dudley so well during his residence in that city. Within forty-eight hours from the failure of Wilson,

Loomis also was among the guests at the Forest, and Thomas was on the alert to give him a good sight at Wales. For this there was again three or four days of anxious watching; a Sunday now intervening, and the young man not venturing into Yarmouth as frequently as usual, Mr. Warner was again on hand to supervise, and his hopes ran high on the coming event.

But I may not weary the indulgence of my readers. The issue in this case was no different from that in Wilson's—Mr. Loomis declared that he had never seen Wales before, and he was certain that Wales was not Dudley. Thus, the problem of his identity was as far from solution as ever—the revelation of the blotting-paper was failing of its high promise!

The identity of Wales with Cone had been so much less likely than with Randall or Dudley, that priority had naturally been given to the settlement of the latter questions. Still, as there is always a possibility in such cases, I now decided to bring on from Philadelphia the blonde young book-keeper who had known the forger as a desk-tenant of Mr. Grattan's. This young gentleman, Mr. Miller, had so frequently seen Cone, and for hours at a time, when he was playing his little game of real-estate agent, that he would undoubtedly be able to tell us whether Wales and he were one. " Send Mr. Miller along," was then the order to Linden.

But while this latest project of identification was pending, Mr. Warner made a discovery at Yarmouth, that gave a new course to all our proceedings. The Superintendent, during his stay, had by no means confined himself to directing the movements of Thomas. Wales was now such a regular visitant, and encountered so many acquaintances in the city, that there was no difficulty in tracing out reputable persons who knew much of him, and would tell what they knew without fear or favor. This field of research was diligently cultivated by Mr. Warner, taking due care that no vestige of a rumor should reach the swindler, that strangers were around who were interested in his antecedents.

Many additional details of his personal history thus became known to us, and all were confirmatory of the opinion we had formed of the man. One little fact, however, transcended all others in its immediate bearing on our operation and its difficulties. This was, that, a few years previously, Wales had been employed as a postal agent, and was on the same route with the very clerk now suspected by Elwell of stealing letters from the mails !

When this jewel of intelligence was flashed into my office at Chicago, a new structure of logic took possession of my thoughts. Special Agent Elwell must be right—that mail-clerk had really stolen the draft letters ; Mr. Bangs must be right—there was a confederacy of mail-thieves, and outside forgers ; and I also was undoubtedly right—Wales was still the very man we wanted!

A mail-clerk who purloined the letters; an outside accomplice to whom he gave them; and forger or forgers who settled down in the cities to prepare for the manipulation of the drafts—such must undoubtedly be the programme of crime!

That blotting-paper, too, was a trump, after all; for had it not brought us to where lay the solution of the mystery?

CHAPTER XV.

Still other startling Swindles.—Severe Measures decided upon.—What the Clicking of a Telegraph Instrument revealed.

THIS new discovery, and the reflections consequent thereon, necessarily led to a new departure. It was needless to attempt further identification of Wales as one of the forgers. He was more likely to be their "go-between" from the spoliators of the mail-bags; and might possibly be the originator of the entire series of depredation. The evidence of any crime on his own part was still entirely wanting; but the conclusion that he was privy to, and participant in, all the mischief accomplished, was now irresistible.

The blonde Mr. Miller was therefore allowed to remain in peace at his desk; and I decided to have Wales arrested on the warrant already obtained, and brought to Philadelphia with a view of "breaking him down;"—a lusty idiom which applies to the detective process of inciting a criminal to divulge the particulars of his crime, and the names of his accomplices.

The intelligence of recent swindles of precisely the same character as those already detained, but of more startling magnitude than any, had also now been communicated to the Agency. I need not at this point burden my narrative with the particulars further than to state that one W. W. Gray had succeeded in collecting nearly twenty thousand dollars on forged drafts in the cities of Troy and Albany, New York State. The period of the thefts and collections agreed very closely with the latest absence of Wales from Redrock, and the amount of money he had on hand at his return suggested a partition of something like this plunder between himself and one or two confederates. Decidedly we must arrest this Wales, take strong grounds with him in regard to the evidence in our possession, and thus "break him down."

And yet, I thought, this man's arrest will be but half our work; and may even defeat the accomplishment of the other half. His capture, once published, would undoubtedly be the signal for his confederates to take flight. It would be very much better, therefore, if I were enabled to clutch them while he was yet at

liberty. His freedom from arrest, for a while longer
at least, is in this view necessary to us. Dudley, or
Randall, or some other, may yet come to confer with
him at Yarmouth, or he go to visit them elsewhere,
and the vigilant Thomas might bag the whole nest—
that is, if Wales does not meanwhile give our detective
the slip, and betake himself from Redrock to parts unknown. The risk of this latter contingency was now
constantly present, and the very thought of it distressing. The only security against it seemed to be the
tenacity of the shadow that attended every morning on
Wales at the Sycamore Valley depot, that flitted after
him unseen through the streets of Yarmouth, and only
forsook him when the evening locomotive rushed westward from the city, bearing him again homeward.
But how feeble, after all, was this grip, on a law-
breaker so sturdy and so guilty as Wales.

This last consideration prevailed over every other.
Thomas had been armed with the warrant, and was
awaiting his final instructions for the arrest of Wales,
when some facts which came to his own knowledge
served to rend away the last tatter of indecision.

One morning he had shadowed his man, as usual,
from the railroad depot into the city. He saw him enter
and leave, in succession, three or four business places ;
apparently engaged in looking after quarry supplies.
He next called in at the General Post-Office, where
of late he had several times received some mail matter.

On all such previous visits Thomas had followed him from the office through the streets, burning with curiosity to know the contents of the letters, which Wales generally perused as he sauntered along. It was the custom of the latter, however, to restore these missives carefully to their envelopes, and deposit them in the breast pocket of his coat ; sometimes even securing them in the recesses of a leather pocket-book.

There was a touch of the methodical Mr. Cone about all this, that was specially exasperating to the inquisitive officer. The correspondence of such a man as Wales must some way hinge upon the secret of his crime ; and the secret of Wales's crime was the objective prize of the detective. And so Thomas had burned and thirsted, but thirsted in vain.

On the particular occasion I refer to, Wales came out of the post-office with two letters in his hand, the address on one of which he was surveying with smiling interest. It was the other one he opened first, however, and read, as was his custom, while moving slowly onward. To the watchful eye of the detective, who was a keen physiognomist, its contents seemed to move Wales considerably ; not as with pain or pleasure, in any of their various forms, did he appear to be affected ; but with the unmistakable impress of *action*—as if the letter prescribed some step of immediate urgency. He folded it up quickly, put it away carefully in his pocket,

6

and at once began to step out with a more rapid and purpose-like stride.

The other letter, which had at first challenged his attention, he now seemed to regard as of only secondary consequence. He tore the envelope open, however, and gave it what seemed to be a most cursory perusal, as he hastily continued his way. His usual wariness also seemed to forsake him, or the exigencies of the moment had made him neglectful. While reading this letter he crumpled up the envelope closely in his hand, and with manifest inadvertence, cast the little ball of paper toward the street gutter. Mr. Thomas, who was walking on the opposite sidewalk, a little in rear of Wales, had marked this action well; and allowing him now to proceed unattended, crossed over the street to make search for the castaway.

After some little trouble he found and picked up the paper, and smoothing it out affectionately, as one might a valuable bank-note, was surprised—if anything could surprise Thomas—to find on it this address :

> **Mr. Harry Norman,**
> Post Office,
> Yarmouth.

This was written in a neat and florid hand, evidently by a lady, the envelope being embossed on the overlap with the text initial L., and having on it the postmark of North Adams, Massachusetts.

That Wales had that morning been somewhat excited by a mail communication; that he was using as an alias the name of Harry Norman; and that he had a lady correspondent in North Adams, who addressed him by that name, were facts of such possible significance that Thomas very properly decided they should be at once made known to the Agency. Before endeavoring to retrace his man, therefore he walked a couple of blocks to a telegraph station to send me the necessary dispatch. To his great satisfaction Wales was in the office before him, and had just finished at a side desk the writing of a dispatch, with which he now went over to the operator, paid the transmission charge, and walked out.

The detective, who was thus far an utter stranger to Wales, had meanwhile hastily engaged in the writing of his own despatch. He continued to write, but not with the same hurry, when the operator had gone in to his instrument, and the jerk of its little handle was shooting out the message of Wales through the slender wires. Although usually a very ready penman, Thomas had now become painfully slow. No chubby-faced school urchin of seven, with tongue thrust in his cheek, could be so desperately deliberate over his first hard copy-line. But withal he kept writing something, writing slowly along—and indeed he wrote rather more than he intended when he came in—while the little telegraph lever went click, clicking, through the silent office, and the trusty, harnessed lightning was bearing the words of Wales some hundreds of miles away !

Having finished his task, the operator was returning to the message counter, when Thomas, as if ashamed of his penmanship, tore in two his labored dispatch, thrust the pieces into his pocket, and hastily left the station. But he did not proceed very far. He simply went to the station of a neighboring telegraph company, and taking out the torn dispatch to copy from, not only transmitted to the Agency the message already determined on, but appended thereto a complete transcript of the message which Wales had just been sending.

The fact was, that during the toilsome task of penmanship I have described, Mr. Thomas had been engaged principally in listening,—his calligraphic agony been merely apparent. He had been listening with feverish intentness to the sounds that issued from the dainty mechanism of the telegraph. Himself a most efficient operator, he possessed the not uncommon facility of reading just as well from the click of the sending key as from the needle movement of the receiving instrument. While the industrious clerk, therefore, was forwarding his customer's dispatch, Thomas was grouping into words the signals that he flung from his finger tips; and not that alone, but writing down those words in careful sequence. In the noiseless office he had found no difficulty in catching every particle of the sound; and when he tore up that paper in such pettish affectation, it contained word for word the entire dispatch of Wales. And this was the dispatch:

" To Miss CARRIE LEVISON,

North Adams, Mass.

" Going East Tuesday evening. Arrange to meet Thursday for trip to Boston. Shall leave a letter for you in post-office. HARRY NORMAN."

The name with which Wales signed this message was the same as that on the envelope he had thrown away in the street, so that his lady correspondent and Miss Carrie Levison were evidently the same person. The motive of Mr. Thomas in sending all the facts to me by a different telegraph line will readily be perceived. It was scarcely necessary to make that guileless operator aware that such very slow writers could have such very quick ears.

CHAPTER XVI.

Wales goes East on a Pleasure-trip. — Mr. Pinkerton furnishes him with exceedingly Attentive Company.

THE time of these occurrences was Monday morning, and Wales returned to Redrock early that afternoon. In the interval he seemed to have been making some hasty visits, as shortly before train-time he stepped rather breathless into the bar-room of the Forest and called for a drink of brandy. Within a few feet of where he stood was the inevitable Thomas, quietly sipping his noon-tide lager, and apparently absorbed in a newspaper which he held up before him. A young city roysterer, who was a frequent visitor at the hotel-bar, gave greeting to Wales, and readily accepted from him a proffered drink. He then urged Wales to join him in a game of billiards. The latter excused himself, evidently on the score of haste, for Thomas could hear a few muttered sentences exchanged in which " Hang the hurry! " received special emphasis. He also overheard the flatulent boast of Wales that he was " going East to see his woman."

" So-so, Mr. Harry Norman," thought the detective, after he had seen his charge seated safely in the cars for Redrock, "so you are going East to forge more drafts, and to have a good time of it with Miss Carrie Levison. Well, I don't rightly know whether you'll get the chance or not, but I think I do know that Mr. Pinkerton will now make up his mind about you. He has given you a pretty loose tether thus far, and I think it's more than likely he'll suddenly bring you up with a round turn."

In these surmises with regard to my course the detective was partly right, and partly wrong. On the receipt of his important advices I did make up my mind, and very promptly too; but not, as he anticipated, to curtail the liberty of Wales. His proposed trip to the East most clearly suggested a better plan. He was now, more than ever, the goose with the golden egg. It would scarcely do to arrest him when perhaps he was on the point of leading me to the very retreat of the forgers. Since it seemed that he himself was neither Dudley, Randall, Davis, nor Cone, these were now the parties I most wanted. I had only been retained, in fact, to bring to justice the forgers who had victimized my employers—the Adams' Express Company. In a certain sense, therefore, Wales had become merely an instrument. But he was a most valuable one, indeed, forasmuch as this fresh journey of his was probably undertaken to meet the forgers, and that new schemes of plunder might be already maturing in some eastern city.

Whether his female correspondent, Carrie Levison, had anything to do with them or not, I had as yet no means of determining. She might equally well be a mere incident in the erratic career of Wales, or a *particeps criminis* in the felonies I was unraveling. Either way we might want her; and for sake of her associations with him, I simply decided that she should be carefully looked after.

This journey, at all events, was the very pink of opportunity for the Agency; and I resolved that no lack, either of precaution or of action, should impede the triumph which I judged to be near at hand. My telegraphic instructions to Thomas, transmitted on Tuesday, were accordingly both full and explicit. He was to travel in the very footsteps of Wales, and shadow him vigilantly wherever he made a pause. In what moment soever he was found in contact with any of his confederates. he and they were to be arrested together. Up to that point, and so long as he held an eastern course, he was to be left in untrammeled liberty ; but if it appeared that he was pushing for the Canadian frontier, he was to be pounced upon at once, whether alone or in company. The same was to be the case if a risk of his escape in any other direction became imminent. A trusty detective, I advised Thomas, would join him at Albany, New York, and assist him in the fulfillment of his now arduous duty. At Boston, in the office of the Adams' Express Company, he would receive his further instructions ; and to the chiefs of the company he would resort for such aid and counsel as sudden emergency might render needful.

Conformably to this part of the programme Mr. Bangs next communicated with Mr. Waldo Adams, advising him of the visitors that might be expected in Boston, and engaging for my detectives and their mission his friendly countenance. I also telegraphed to Bangs to have a competent detective sent on to Albany to meet Mr. Thomas, and act under his orders— if an officer who was personally known to him, so much the better.

In the course of the forenoon I was gratified by the intelligence that Mr. W. E. Delancy had been assigned to that duty, he being just the manner of man to answer its requirements—vigilant, active, and fearless to a degree. There was no telling what kind of tough work our men would have on hand, when they succeeded in tracking the plunderers to their den. Finally, I advised Thomas of the selection of his associate, and where he might expect to see him.

The same morning Wales and his father came into Yarmouth in company. The former had with him a valise and trunk, and his first proceeding was to have them checked at the baggage office for Troy, N. Y. By a simple ruse Thomas ascertained this immediately after he stepped out, and then he started to follow the pair cautiously. The younger Wales was gayly attired, and evidently in high spirits; the smirk of self-conceit, and the smile of fancied pleasures, chasing each other by turns over his not unhandsome countenance. He made profuse display of his loud watch-chain, and diamond studs and breast-pin, and all the rest of his foppish belongings; and he tripped along the street with the air of a spangled showman. Father and son together made several business calls; and then loitered around among their acquaintance in a pleasant and gossipy way. Thomas was never far distant from them throughout the entire day.

Among other things he observed that the highly

6*

respectable Mayor of Redrock showed no manner of distrust as to the destination of his son. No grave and prolix advice, or stern admonition, seemed to engage the paternal tongue. He simply deported himself as a sire who had come to town to give his boy a send-off, and then to circulate and enjoy himself after the fashion of his years. Whether conscious or not of his son's criminal pursuits—and in charity we must presume not—he exhibited no outward sign. Thomas could even fancy, as he pictured in his report, that " there was a chuckle in the old man's voice, and a satisfied twinkle in his eye, as if secretly he gloated over Willie's success." The questionable methods of this success seemed not to concern him.

In the course of the day the young man drew a check at the bank for five hundred dollars, payable to his divorced wife,—a lady who still resided in the vicinity of Yarmouth. He also called in at the depot and bought a sleeping-car ticket for Rochester. Then tor a further while he strutted jauntily around, as if his heart were all guiltless, and his pockets all crammed with the gains of honest effort. No glimmer of apprehension seemed to dawn upon him that the Nemesis of justice was fast upon his heels.

At five o'clock in the afternoon Wales had given "good-bye" to his father, and was comfortably seated in the eastward-bound train. So, also, toward the rear of the same car, was Mr. J. R. Thomas, a timid-looking, student-like man, who wore glasses, and was constantly engaged with a rusty-covered volume he had taken from his pocket. Although absolute disguise was unnecessary, and not attempted by him, the officer was a very different-looking person from the frank and cordial gentleman who had been prospecting among the Redrock quarries. He knew not how often or how long he might wish to be near Wales, without in any way attracting the notice of the latter. A person who should be frequently encountered by the swindler during his trip—however unsuspicious-looking, would infallibly cause him some uneasiness. Every little change of aspect and demeanor was therefore a gain to Thomas ; variety being concealment sufficient for his purpose. The mere removal of his glasses and wig would be disguise enough at a further stage of his journey.

Whether the detective was entirely absorbed by the contents of that rusty volume the reader is at liberty to doubt; although it was no other than an old copy of Irving's delightful *Sketch Book*, and Thomas is a person both of taste and culture. He had just finished reading, for the tenth time in his life, perhaps, the quaint old " Legend of Sleepy Hollow," when Wales betook himself yawning into his compartment. Thomas went to his berth also, and being much fatigued, slept quite soundly ; nor did he awake until the morning sun was peering through the carriage windows, as the train swept along through the woods of western New York.

It was now indeed a lovely morning, and Nature had arrayed the earth as if crime or sorrow had no place upon its surface; as if forgers and detectives were beings of another planet. A fresh fall of snow had covered during the night the unsightly blotches left by a recent thaw. The bare branches of the trees, down to the veriest twig, were laden and fringed with its fleecy wealth. Field and river-bank, woodland and slope, were sheeted all over in its stainless white. And from a clear blue sky the sun flashed its radiance around and over all, till the land appeared lustrous as a happy bride.

What sentiments this fair prospect may have inspired in the breast of the swindler, Thomas knew nor cared not. The mind of the criminal is unfitted to rejoice in the beauties of nature, for these only address themselves to clean hearts. The detective observed that after Wales had made his toilet, he sat down and looked forth sullenly from the glistening carriage window. The sole diversion, indeed, that he seemed to find in these morning hours, was the detention for breakfast at Rochester, after which he brightened with some of his wonted assurance.

In the depot at the city named he encountered a man with whom he took a drink, and who parted from him with a " Good-bye, Harry !" At Syracuse, also,

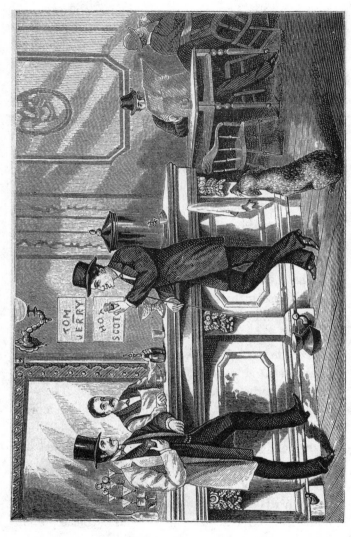

*A young city roysterer * * * * accepted from him a proffered drink.*

he had a couple of drinks with another man, who came aboard the train, and continued in close converse with Wales as far as Schenectady, where he left. There was nothing in the appearance of either of those men to correspond with the descriptions that had been furnished to Thomas of the forgers. The latter, therefore, resumed his rusty volume, and continued to read, and to watch.

At two o'clock in the afternoon the train reached Albany, and even before alighting, the detective recognized on the platform the punctual Delaney. While the passengers were crowding about, he managed to give his associate a good "spot" on Wales. It was then hastily arranged that they should both now shadow him, but separately, and with independent vigilance; only coming together when the opportunities for conference were entirely free from risk.

Almost immediately Wales took a train for Troy, a distance of but six miles from Albany. The two detectives were in the same car with him, but quite undistinguishable from the average Albanians and Trojans by whom it was filled. At Troy Wales descended, and took dinner at the American House, whence he emerged soon after and proceeded to the Union Depot. Here he had his baggage re-checked for North Adams, Massachusetts.

The five o'clock train took the same parties to North Adams, where, shortly after seven, Mr. "Harry Norman,

Yarmouth, Ohio," had registered at the Wilson House, and was partaking of a toothsome supper.

The detectives now relieved each other to procure some needed refreshment, and it was gathered from their reports that Wales spent about two hours after supper in watching out upon the street from the corridor of the hotel. Whoever it was that he expected he seemed not to discover, for about ten o'clock he retired to his room, evidently for the night.

Delaney had engaged his room, and also slept at the Wilson House. Thomas found quarters in a hotel across the street.

CHAPTER XVII.

One of the Gentler Sex appears.— Wales and Carrie Levison, at North Adams, Mass., indulge in a Sleigh-ride.—A Shrewd and Tricky Couple.

FOR the first time there now appears among the characters of this story one of the gentler sex. If I were writing a mere work of fiction, it would be my privilege, and might be my pleasure, to endow her with such moral graces as would attract the reader's regard. But mine is a tale of a very prosaic and wicked world. The characters, incidents, and situations are all a series of still recent facts; nor may I palliate the wrong, or put a gloss over the moral turpitude that became manifest during this operation. The heroine I must introduce, then, though indeed fair to behold, was simply one who had forgotten the precepts of maidenly honor, or had become so demoralized through the vanities of female dress as to place her fair fame in the keeping of the swindler, Wales.

The morning after his arrival at the Wilson House "Mr. Harry Norman" was stirring betimes. His approaching meeting with Carrie was having an inspiriting effect on him. His appearance gave evidence of a painstaking toilet; and he walked into the breakfast-room with a beaming countenance. He made quite a hearty meal of it, too ; but, in this as in everything else, found means for the display of his egregious vanity. He inflicted more petty complaints, and made more needless trouble to the waiter, than some jaded city epicure who had a million to support his caprices. The chicken was broiled to a crust, the biscuits were underdone, the coffee, the butter, and all the rest, were not fit to eat.

After the manner of his race and profession, the Ethiopian waiter endured this tirade with grinning good-humor. It also amused a gentleman who was seated at another table, somewhat in rear of Wales, making quiet but rapid demolition of a ponderous beefsteak. This person was Mr. Delaney, whose resolute assaults on the "short sirloin," as is frequently the case with detectives, were inspired by the uncertainty as to the time for another meal.

Immediately after his breakfast Wales went into the reading-room and wrote a letter. Then he put on his great-coat, and a pair of rubber overshoes, and sallied forth from the hotel. His first move was in the direction of the post-office, where, instead of mailing his letter in the ordinary drop, he handed it in over the counter with the explanation that the lady to whom it was addressed would speedily call. This insured its being at once placed in the proper compartment for delivery.

Within the little inclosure which contained the postmaster's desk, Mr. Thomas was seated at that very moment. The intention of Wales to deposit a letter for Miss Levison was already known to him; so on that point there was nothing new to be learned. His immediate purpose there was to obtain from a reliable source some information about that lady herself. For this he had called in early on the postmaster—an obliging little gentleman—and without declaring his precise business in North Adams, satisfied him that it was legitimate, and even related to the service of the department. Thereupon the functionary made no hesitation in telling the officer, as might any other citizen, the little that he knew of Miss Carrie Levison.

She was the daughter, he said, of an old resident of the place, who was a storekeeper by occupation, but only in a small way of business. Having received a good education she was a clever and ladylike person; and her bright, genial disposition had made her a general favorite with those who knew her. From the time she was a growing girl—and she was still quite young—the postmaster had remembered her coming to the office for her own and the family letters. Recently, for about a year or so, she was away from North Adams; and only within the last few weeks did she appear to be again residing with her father. Somebody, he thought, had told him that she was employed during that period as a teacher of a local school in some town on the Connecticut River.

It was at this point that Wales brought in his letter, and when he had left the office the postmaster exclaimed to Thomas:

"Why, there's a letter, I declare, for the very young lady you are interested in—and left by a stranger too."

Before noticing the remark Thomas glanced quickly out of the window; but, as he saw Mr. Delaney industriously kicking the snow from his boots at an opposite doorstep, he knew that Wales could not go far astray.

"Miss Levison has a good many visitors and letters, I suppose?" now inquired the detective.

"No; I rather think not," answered the postmaster; "though I judge there must be more than one young fellow round here who would be proud to bask in her smiles. She seems quite select in her company, how ever, and dresses almost as well as any lady in North Adams; indeed, I have often wondered how her father could afford to give her such a stylish outfit."

"But what about her general conduct and reputation?"

"So far as I know, they are all that could be desired," said the postmaster warmly; "Carrie is really a sweet, handsome little lady, and seems fitted to adorn almost any sphere."

Mr. Thomas here expressed his thanks to the official, and after a brief exchange of commonplace, gave him a polite good-morning, and left the office.

Proceeding in the direction of the hotel he soon encountered his brother detective, and learned from him that Wales had just entered the office of a livery stables, beyond the corner of the adjacent block. Both now loitered around, and in about fifteen minutes' time the object of their attentions was seen driving out of the stables in a gayly-appointed cutter, with a handsome buffalo-robe spread out before him. He had a lively bay horse in hand, which he steered proudly along to the door of the Wilson House. There he alighted, and passing the lines to an attendant porter, skipped into the hotel as for a brief call.

The opportunity was not lost on Thomas. He promptly ran to the same livery stables, procured another sleigh, and drove quickly back to where Delaney remained watching Wales.

"He's been getting out a shawl, I think, and some creature comforts," remarked the latter detective; "I saw him stow away something like that under the seat of the cutter."

"Going for a ride with his girl, no doubt," returned Thomas, as he held back the sleigh-robe to let Delaney in beside him; "jump in and let us see if this old nag can't keep 'em in sight."

"Don't fear for that," answered Delaney, pleasantly. "If he don't do the respectable we must give him some whip-sauce!—either a three-minute pace or a scarred horse-hide—that's the way to do it."

For a while at least this fierce alternative was not found to be necessary. Wales drove round and about lazily through the principal streets, as if merely design-ing a survey of their attractions. The traffic was now quite lively, and the merry jangle of the sleigh-bells was heard in every direction. From the cumbrous sleds of the grocer and butcher to the dainty little chariot of the pleasure-seeker, the vehicles dashed hither and thither over the crisp snow. The detect-ives had no difficulty in keeping Wales in view, nor much fear that he should specially notice them—for his attention was fully absorbed by the management of his horse. At last the swindler seemed to take a look at his watch, after which he turned into a quiet avenue, and drove more rapidly towards the eastern outskirts of the village.

" Appointment for ten o'clock, I'll bet," said Thomas to his companion, looking at his own watch, by which he saw it wanted but a few minutes of that hour.

To all appearance the detective was right. On the eastern road from North Adams Wales drew up his cutter by the side-walk, where a lady stood waiting. As he jumped out and greeted her warmly, and then busied himself with fixing for her accommodation the sleigh-robe and shawl, the detectives drove slowly past, making a keen inspection of Miss Carrie Levison, for that was the lady herself. A bright-faced, pretty-looking creature she was, in the first flush of womanhood, with a pyramid of glossy black hair piled up under her jaunty little hat. A pouting, cherry ripe mouth; large, lustrous black eyes, under perfect brows; plump features of exquisite regularity; and a complexion rosy with health, and beaming with animation—completed the picture of a Hebe that might tempt St. Anthony. She was quite below the average height of woman withal, but had the easy grace and carriage of good breeding; and was very seasonably attired in a tasteful dark suit, and good set of furs. She realized well, in short, the worthy postmaster's summary, and looked every inch " a sweet, handsome little lady."

In a very few moments the cutter overtook and dashed past the officers, the swindler being seated close up to Miss Levison, and apparently oblivious of every-

The cutter overtook and dashed past the officers.

thing save her musical chatter. The road led out in the direction of the Hoosac Tunnel, but no curious inspection of that great work seemed to occur to the mind of Wales. Nor dreamed he either, as it seemed, that the sleuth-hounds of the law were close in his tracks, and that his career of crime and folly was fast drawing to an end. The " fair defect of nature " at his side had now enchained him in bondage most absolute. The fear that clings to guilt was vanquished in her smiles, and pleasure reigned supreme, the monarch of the hour.

But we may not loiter too long with this unblest pair. After a three hours' excursion they returned to the village, the two detectives being close behind. Carrie was let down at a quiet corner of the avenue, and wended her homeward way on foot. Wales then put up his sleigh at the livery stables and returned into the Wilson House.

At four o'clock the swindler again left the hotel, and, accompanied by his baggage, got aboard the train for Pittsfield. Thomas and Delaney went separately into the same car, and exchanged a swift glance of intelligence as they simultaneously noted that Carrie Levison was already seated therein. She was not near Wales, however, and no sign of recognition seemed to pass between them.

Arrived at Pittsfield the whole party got out, and Wales bought two tickets for Boston, still keeping apart from his enticing fellow-traveler. As the passengers crowded into the Boston cars, he lagged a little behind the rest. So, too, did the anxious Mr. Thomas. Delaney, meanwhile, had gone in after Carrie, and taking a back seat, was soon to all appearance fascinated by his newspaper. Not quite so fascinated, however, but that he noticed Wales, as he came down the aisle, drop one of the Boston tickets in Carrie's lap. He then took a lower seat on the opposite side, and did not approach the girl until the train was about twenty miles on its journey. In this distance many passengers had come and gone, and he now ventured into the same seat with her, and chatted away as with a newly-made acquaintance.

At Springfield the pair had supper together, and then resumed the same seat until the train reached Palmer Junction. When the cars stopped here, Miss Levison quitted her companion, and got out, the latter exhibiting no sign of a like intention. Their parting had been so unceremonious, however, that Thomas suspected a trick, and motioned to the other detective to hold fast.

As soon as the train had fairly started, Wales sprang up from his seat, went out on the front platform, and dropped off the car.

In an instant Thomas was at Delaney's side.

"Just as I thought," he said quickly; "going to stop here over night. You drop off and stick by 'em,

I'll go to Boston for our dispatches. Telegraph the Agency how it is; and look out for me at the depot when you come."

Rapid as thought Delaney went through the same door as Wales, but only swung himself off when the train had passed out of the shed, and he knew he would be unseen by the tricky fugitive. The increasing speed of the cars, and the fact that he had to jump down on the road-bed, made it a performance of considerable risk, but I have already stated that Delaney was an intrepid officer.

In the main street of Palmer he came up with Wales and Carrie, the former all smiles and confidence, now having the girl on his arm. At the Otawaso House they had soon registered their names as " Harry Norman and wife, Cleveland, Ohio," and very shortly after both retired to their room.

Mr. Delaney sent a brief telegram to the Agency, and once more slept soundly under the same roof with the criminal.

CHAPTER XVIII.

In Boston.—The Detectives locate themselves in Close Companion-ship to the Gay Couple.—Wales, in his fancied Security, makes Damaging Confessions.—Other interesting Facts and Incidents.

THE following morning Wales and his young mistress came down early to breakfast. When that was dispatched he procured a sleigh and drove out with Carrie a few miles into the country. The weather had become colder, and the rude gusts from the North whirled the snow around them in spiteful gusts. But they chatted and laughed with all the gayety of youth and innocence ; while the girl was heard to remark that the day was " perfectly splendid !"

On the road, near Palmer, they outdistanced another sleigh, which had left the village at a more lively pace ; and again they passed it when returning. Neither of them, however, condescended a glance at the mean-look-ing, muffled-up occupant, whose hat was tied down over his ears, and whose nose was the reddest and most dis-tinguished of his features. Yet that person was their faithful shadow, Delaney ; and though he did not feel much like sleigh-riding that morning, his trip lasted quite as long as theirs—and no longer.

At two o'clock in the afternoon Wales and Carrie took the Boston train, on which they occupied an end compartment of a drawing-room car. The detective disposed himself on a seat in the main section, having merely taken care that it was in full view of the door of said compartment. Without any incident worth noting the party arrived in Boston shortly before six o'clock—only one of the number knowing that the young gentleman who lounged about in the depot was Mr. J. R. Thomas, also a recent arrival from Northern Ohio. That gentleman lounged to some purpose, too, for he managed to be near enough to the hack which Wales and Carrie had entered, to hear the order given to drive to the Revere House. The detectives at once took a hack to themselves, and were deposited in the same hotel just in time to see Wales turn away from the register, and pass up the staircase with Carrie by the hand.

On the register it was found that " H. Norman and wife, Toledo, Ohio," had been assigned to room No. 156 ; and the names of Messrs. Thomas of Philadelphia and Delaney of New York soon appeared boldly a little further down.

Early that morning, before it became advisable to go to the railroad depot, Mr. Thomas had called for his letters at the office of the Adams' Express Company. There he received and acknowledged my latest dispatches, from which his instructions had been elaborated by the General Superintendent. My opinion being that Wales had gone East to meet some of his con-

7

federates, and pass more drafts, Thomas was enjoined
to be fully on the alert, and shadow every movement
that took place in Boston. He was to do this pati
ently, as it might take several days for the swindler to
get in contact with his friends, and accomplish the collection of the drafts. He and they were then to be
arrested, with the plunder on them if possible, and
taken red-handed to the Agency at Philadelphia.

At half past seven o'clock, the evening of their
arrival, Wales and Carrie took a hack at the Revere
House and proceeded to the Boston Theater. Delaney
was close behind them in a similar vehicle, and only
left them when they were snugly ensconced in the re-
served chairs, and the performance had entered on the
second act. At its conclusion he was again on hand to
see them back to the hotel, and almost to their very
room.

On the morrow the pair went to a matinee at the
Boston Museum, and in the evening to the Howard
Athenæum; remaining in each case to the end of the
entertainment, and carefully shadowed both out and
back. The next forenoon they had a long carriage
ride, round the harbor and in the suburbs, and in the
evening they went to a performance at the Globe
Theater; Thomas bringing up the rear during the
carriage excursion, and Delaney regaling himself with
melodrama at the Globe.

But however diverting to Wales and the pretty

young sinner from North Adams, this routine of pastimes was most wearisome to the officers. A grave responsibility reposed in their hands, and they were itching to see their task to a safe termination. During the three days since his arrival in Boston, Wales had neither made any calls, met any acquaintance, nor held any visible correspondence that would indicate a purpose to adventure in his nefarious business. The conviction began to impress itself on his unseen watchers that he had merely come East for "a big jamboree;" or, as Thomas suggested in one of his pithy reports—"to cater to the lascivious pleasings of the frail Carrie."

On the day last chronicled, therefore, that energetic officer decided to make a sort of advance on the enemy's works. In reconnoitring through the Revere House he had ascertained that room No. 157, adjoining the apartment of "Harry Norman and wife," had been some time unoccupied. A brief examination also showed him that a person in either of those apartments could hear almost every word that was clearly spoken in the other. On a pretense that he and his New York friend, Mr. Delaney, were desirous of a room of just that size, he procured the hotel clerk to transfer them to No. 157. When Delaney came home from the theater, shadowing Wales and Carrie, his associate informed him of the change of quarters, and urged that on retiring they should make as little noise as possible, so their neighbors might not perceive that the room had found tenants.

" I shall say my prayers in a whisper rather than disturb them ;" was the response of the accommodating Delaney.

The weather next morning proved to be quite unpleasant. Squalls of easterly wind, and tormenting showers of sleet and rain, gave token of the advancing season; while they also confined within doors the average promenader of Boston. As usual Mr. Thomas went out early to the office of the Express Company, to look after his dispatches. Wales and Carrie had breakfast served in their room; and Delaney sat quietly in his new quarters, smoking and listening.

The detective soon heard from the next room the sharp popping of a champagne cork, and the soft gurgle of the wine as it was poured out. Very soon after his neighbors seemed to become loquacious; and from the exclamations and fragments of sentences that reached him, he could gather that Wales was in the mood confidential. At this Delaney seated himself closer to the partition, and easily discerned that the swindler was relating some of his criminal achievements. The frankness with which he spoke, too, and the frivolous, unchiding interruptions of his companion, made it entirely evident that she was already informed of his felonious pursuits.

The room occupied by the guilty pair, and the one

in which the detective had ensconced himself, had evidently been used *en suite*, at some former time, and were still separated by folding doors, the upper part of which were fitted with ground-glass panes for admitting light, but excluding sight. Within the upper row of these panes there had been a light broken which was replaced by an unground light; so that by quietly moving his table to this door, placing a chair upon the table, and then mounting this structure, Delaney could not only look down upon the apparently happy couple, but also hear every word of their conversation, which was of far more importance, for it was an hour of revelations and confidences between the fascinating couple at their dainty little breakfast; and he lost no time in availing himself of this new and unexpected advantage.

At one time Wales exclaimed :

" If I was pulled now I am gone up !"

Further on he was heard to say, evidently after the narration of some boasted exploit :

" It took a long time to work the job right, at least four months, and a good deal of study ; I thought at one time my chances weren't worth a red."

And again he remarked :

" I wouldn't like to have been caught, though, for I don't like to disgrace the folks at home; and I don't fancy hard work either, or learning a new trade ;" his meaning in the latter allusion being clearly that he did not relish a sojourn in prison.

The clink of the bottle and glasses, and the pleasant clatter of the dishes was here again heard, and at the same moment Thomas re-entered the room in which Delaney was perched eavesdropping. The latter instantly raised his finger to his lips as an admonition to silence, and, apprehending the position at once, Thomas took a chair and sat down at one side of the table, facing him, and also close to the partition. He likewise manifested his interest in the situation, by taking out his memorandum book and pencil, and placing them on his knee like a reporter at a campaign meeting.

It was evident that their neighbors had not heard the entrance of Thomas, for Wales now launched out in a more reliant tone, and began to favor Carrie with reminiscences of his past life. He spoke of the time when he was a mail agent on the eastern route; and of his having frequently opened money letters and appropriated their contents.

" I can tell," said he boastfully, and therefore quite distinctly, " by the feeling of them whether there is any money in them. If there were a hundred letters in a package, and ten of them contained money, I could pick out the whole ten without a single mistake."

" How *could* you tell, Harry ?" was here the inquiry of the interested Miss Levison.

" Oh ! practice makes perfect, you know," was the satisfactory explanation of Wales ; and then he added : " The ' cops ' were put on me and Hobart and another chap, for awhile ; but they couldn't catch *me* napping. I used to 'tumble to them' regular whenever they come into our car, and if there was any noise about a lost money letter I could shove the suspicion on some of the others. One time, however, there was a cop named Wright that figured me down pretty close ; but I gave him the very haul I was after making, to settle the whole matter with him."

The two detectives exchanged glances at this entertaining, and, to them, intelligible story. They did not need to be told, though my readers will, that "cop" means a detective, and to "tumble to" a person, is to recognize him in his real character, both expressions being slang of the kind that is current among thieves. Only Mr. Delaney, however, ventured on a whispered remark, in reference to the bribery of the "cop named Wright."

"Them's your municipal kind !" were all the words he said.

But Wales had not quite finished his disclosures. He next spoke of a man who had come into the mail-car one day, passing right by Hobart to where he was standing, and said, "I am the United States Marshal." The remainder of this incident did not penetrate to the ears of the detectives, but its conclusion was heard in the chuckling boast of the thief—"And I had over a dozen letters in my pocket at the very time ; I could take all I wanted, indeed, even if the cops were in the very car with me."

From these unedifying memories the swindler once more returned to the present; and he blithely informed Miss Carrie that "settling down" was a step he had now finally resolved on. He next recalled to the hapless girl the numerous good things he had lately done for her! He catalogued with atrocious fidelity all the presents he had made her, both in dress and trinkets, and also the sums of money he had given her—and even went so far as to figure up the exact total for her, at $593. But even this incredible baseness went quite unrebuked by his callous little victim—there occurring to her no better than this mercenary suggestion:

"Well, I think now, Harry, that you might as well give me the other seven dollars, and make it the even six hundred!"

She turned her pouting lips up towards him and reached out her pretty white hand as she said this, seeming the incarnation of deviltry and sweetness. He paramour looked at her admiringly for a moment, and then flung her a bill of large denomination, which, with a merry little burst of laughter, she put in her bosom for a temporary receptacle, in a very business-like way, when the breakfast and the conversation was resumed.

The detectives were not sorry when this singular conversation was ended; which it now was, by Wales

"You might as well give me the other seven dollars, and make it even six hundred!"

jumping up and proposing a carriage ride. The girl agreed quite readily; and a few moments later the officers heard them pass through the corridor on their way down-stairs. Delaney at once started out to follow them in a hack; while Thomas hastened to the telegraph office to transmit to the Agency the essence of their morning's conversation.

Early the same afternoon, and while the shadowed pair were still out of doors, Thomas was informed by the hotel Superintendent—to whom he had confided just an inkling of his business—that the Ohio gentleman and his wife, who roomed next door to him, were leaving for the West by the night express.

"For the West, did you say, sir?" inquired the detective eagerly.

"Yes, sir; Mr. Norman told me they were about returning home," answered the obliging potentate of the Revere.

This important news was instantly transmitted to the Philadelphia Agency; Mr. Linden having been specially intrusted with the management of Wales' arrest. Before two hours the detectives were in receipt of that gentleman's instructions. The fruit was at last ripe for plucking, but it was not to be gathered in Boston. The officers were to accompany Wales on his westward journey, but not to arrest him until they had crossed the Pennsylvania State line, and were approaching Erie. Himself and the lady were then to be hur-

7*

ried to Philadelphia, separately, if possible, but no risk was to be taken on her account as to the security of the swindler himself.

The reader will perceive the motive of this arrangement when he recalls that the warrant of arrest had been obtained in Philadelphia, on depositions of an offense committed in that city. If Wales were arrested outside of Pennsylvania, the processes required to authorize his removal might involve some delay, and would certainly be attended with wide publicity— while neither delay nor publicity could at this point be tolerated.

The arrest of Miss Levison had been determined on at my own suggestion—that not being the wife of Wales, she was really a *particeps criminis.* Even if not finally arraigned, she could be held as an accessory in his crimes; and she might prove a valuable instrument in breaking him down, and perhaps in discovering to us the other criminals.

So far, at least, as W. R. Wales was concerned, the course of our operation now seemed clear.

CHAPTER XIX.

*Wales and Carrie Levison, accompanied by their two Invisible At-
tendants, leave Boston——A dark Shadow of Apprehension.——
The final Arrest of Wales.*

BUT the swindler did not carry out his intention of
leaving Boston that night. Once more he went
to the theater with Carrie; and this time Mr. Delaney
sat out a very tedious performance to watch him; while
Thomas attended his exit to shadow him to the hotel.
The idea had occurred to the detectives that, on this last
night of his stay, he might still endeavor to communicate with his confederates.

No such proceeding transpired, however, and in the
morning, quite early, the detectives could distinguish
from his room the notes of preparation. At eight o'clock
Wales had settled up his hotel-bill, and shortly afterwards left the Revere in a hack; the baggage of himself and Carrie, which accompanied them, giving assurance of their final exodus. The detectives were, of
course, in marching order, and followed closely behind.

At the Boston and Albany depot Wales bought two
tickets for the last-named city; and Detective Thomas
did the same. The swindler next had himself and his
companion booked for adjacent chairs in a drawing-room
car. Ere they were well seated therein, Mr. Delaney
was reclining at length on a sofa-seat in the same section.

Mr. Thomas, opposite the trio, was assiduously drying the window-pane with his pocket-handkerchief, that he might feast without hindrance on the sweet desolation of the landscape.

No incident worthy of record befell them during this trip, until the party reached Albany at three o'clock in the afternoon. The same as in Boston, Mr. " H. Norman and wife," of Yarmouth, O., were speedily registered at the Delavan House ; and not knowing what stay they intended, their faithful shadows followed the example.

From the moment Wales and Carrie retired to their room, there was no movement on their part to give further occupation to the officers. It was known that they came down to the dining-room for their meals, and that was all.

At two o'clock the next afternoon the pair descended to the ladies' parlor, and at the ticket agency in the hotel Wales purchased a single ticket for North Adams, and had Carrie's trunk re-checked for that destination. He then accompanied her to the cars, where he seated her quite tenderly ; and just as the train was about starting gave her a warm shake-hands and a farewell kiss.

The detectives had been lurking near, quite ready to jump on the train if Wales had remained in the cars, They now followed him back to the Delavan, and no ticed, as they did, that he was already a changed man. The illusory gleam of pleasure had given place on his countenance to the dark shadows of apprehension. His brief interval of revelry at an end, he seemed again remitted to the companionship of his guilt; and he looked and moved—

"As if his fear still followed him behind!"

In the marble corridors of the Delavan he now walked up and down during a weary half hour. But he was entirely wrapt up in his own sinister mood, and quite unobservant of the turmoil around him—for it was that season of Albany law-making when the Delavan becomes a Babel as "the outer lobby" of the State Capitol. The honorable and dishonorable legislators of the Empire State were caucusing and conspiring in groups all around him; but he heard not their voices, and heeded not their presence. The scheming lobbyists jostled him time and again, as they glided to and fro on their missions of corruption, but Wales continued his promenade with averted glance and nervous self-abstraction. He could scarcely have shown greater prostration, indeed, had he known the fact that one of those two stalwart men, who were smoking and chatting on a velveted hall-seat, had the warrant for his arrest in a convenient pocket. Yet so it was.

At last the thief turned into the bar-room, and having gulped down a large drink of brandy, walked quickly back to the office, like one who had torn himself from indecision into settled purpose. Here he paid

his bill, and directed a porter to bring down his
trunk and valise, and have the articles checked for
Toledo at once. This having been done, and the baggage sent over to the depot, he hastened out himself to
the western-bound train, and promptly took his seat in
a drawing-room car. So, likewise, did the pertinacious
officers ; and in little more than an hour from his parting with Carrie, they were again his fellow-travelers—
watchful of him, yet unheeded ; strangers to him, yet
instruments in his fate.

It was half past three o'clock when the train started,
but no change occurred until its arrival at Rochester in
the evening, when Wales got out and took a berth in a
sleeping coach. The detectives paid for a section in
the same car, but not by any means to use it as a sleeping apartment. Even had they been thus disposed,
sleep would have vanished from their eyelids, at the
thought of the approaching consummation of their important duty. In the dim light of the section they sat
whispering in a low key, as the train thundered along
in the darkness, only peeping out during its stoppages
to assure themselves there was no movement of the
occupant of No. 4—the section in which the thief had
his berth. The latter, however, appeared to sleep
soundly throughout the night.

It wanted but little of four o'clock in the morning
when the locomotive crossed the New York State line
and entered Pennsylvania—-rattling along at a good

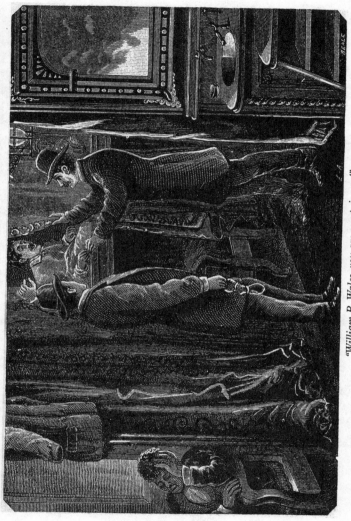

"William R. Wales, you are our prisoner!"

speed towards Erie. Without a moment's delay the two detectives got up and passed into No. 4 Section Wales, who was its only occupant, was still in a deep sleep, but Thomas shook him sturdily by the shoulder till he awoke.

" Who is it ?—what do you want ?" said the swindler snappishly, as he looked up with a dazed expression at the intruders.

"William R. Wales, you are our prisoner," answered Thomas, in a low, distinct voice, but without taking his hand from the reclining man.

He added:

" Now, if you want to get through without making a sensation for the railroad folks—and I rather think you do—you will just spring up and dress yourself at once ; we shall be at Erie in a few minutes, and we must take you off the cars there."

"What for ?—where's your warrant ?" demanded Wales with tolerable composure, although his eyes still gleamed as in a conflict of surprise and vexation.

" You are going straight to Philadelphia under a warrant sworn out in that city—just listen to it a moment, and then hurry up."

In a rapid but quiet manner Mr. Thomas here read to him the warrant of arrest, omitting only the aliases under which his prisoner was named. Recognizing, apparently, that all was in due form, and that the least hesitation would only bring about a most hateful exposure, Wales promptly stood up and proceeded to don his attire.

The obliging Mr. Delaney stood by, to hand him, as required, each article of clothing—only first searching the pockets to discover any papers or other articles of which it might be prudent to relieve him. The first thing found was a small Smith and Wesson revolver, which was loaded, and which Thomas secured on his own person. All the papers the thief had about him seemed to be in a stout pocket-book, which was taken from the breast of his coat. The removal of this article, and its transfer to the pocket of Thomas, appeared to cast a cloud over the face of his prisoner; but he gave no voice to his discontent, and every moment became more collected. His watch, and money—of which there was about three hundred dollars—with other articles of no special significance, were left undisturbed in his pockets. The whole affair had transpired within a few minutes, and so quietly as to attract no notice from other persons on the train.

But the outskirts of Erie had now been reached, and Thomas sent his brother detective to the baggage agent to have the check for his prisoner's trunk exchanged for a Philadelphia one. This was immediately done; and when the cars stopped at the depot the thief had a most effectual escort in the brace of sturdy officers between whom he passed into the street.

Wales was at once brought to the Ellsworth House,

and taken into a private room, to await the departure of the Philadelphia Express, which would start from Erie about a quarter past eight. Here the whole party took breakfast, and Thomas embraced the opportunity to write up his reports, and to telegraph to the several Agency offices that he was at last in possession of his prisoner, who might be expected in Philadelphia about noon of that day.

During the detention at the Ellsworth the swindler recovered somewhat his usual self-assurance, although he spoke but little, and that only in reply to the observations of his captors. When Thomas made a reference to the serious difficulty in which his crimes had entangled him, he smiled in affected derision, and said:

"Pshaw! that's all stuff; I have done no crimes against the law, except to make a bit of money by gambling, and your mighty Mr. Pinkerton will know that before long!"

"Well," observed the detective, "Mr. Pinkerton is just the man to give you a chance, if he finds there are worse in the crowd than you are."

To this remark Wales made no answer, but Thomas could fancy from his countenance that he had listened to it not without interest.

At train-time the officers and their prisoner again went aboard the cars, and were soon speeding along by the Philadelphia ard Erie Railroad towards the Quaker City. By direction of Thomas, Mr. Delaney occupied the same seat with Wales, the latter being next the car window; while Thomas took to himself the next seat behind, which was close enough to permit, if so minded, of his hearing and joining in their conversation.

From Corry, the first station at which they stopped, the detective again sent brief telegrams to Chicago. New York and Philadelphia, to apprise the Agency that he was now fairly *en route*. During the entire trip the prisoner was quite tractable and gentlemanly, and chatted freely on almost any subject save that of the crimes imputed to him. Taking advantage of an earnest talk in which Delaney engaged him, Thomas now made a hasty inspection of the book which had been taken from his breast pocket. Apparently it was a memorandum book, or business diary—if crime may be expressed as a business—and was all in the handwriting of Wales, but disguised in a cipher which the officer failed to interpret. In the pockets of the cover were a number of photographs of Carrie Levison, taken at Delevan, Ohio; three or four cabinet pictures of Wales by a Cleveland photographer, and some business cards of tailors, jewelers and other tradesmen, in cities East and West.

Of all the entries in the book itself, a list of addresses, which filled three or four pages, alone was traced in ordinary writing. To the officer, however, it was supremely interesting, for it included such familiar names as, "R. D. Randall, Newark, N. J.;" "Randall & Co.,

Grand Rapids, Mich. ;" "Wales and Reed, Clyde, Ohio ;" "R. W. Davis" and "Miss Lizzie Greenleaf, at Dunstable Bros., No. — Wood street, Pittsburg," which last the reader may recall as the name of Dudley's sister-in-law.

Shortly before noon the party arrived in Philadelphia, and Wales was removed quickly to the Agency, in an upper room of which a dinner had been provided. This he partook in the society of his captors and fellow-travelers of the morning.

CHAPTER XX.

Mr. Bangs Decides to make a Thief Assist in Catching a Forger— "Breaking" Wales "Down."

IN a very few minutes after the arrival of Wales at the Agency, its threshold was also crossed by my General Superintendent, Mr. Bangs, who had come from New York by the morning's express. For several nights previous, in connection with other operations, he had been continuously on the wing. Landing at New York, after a tedious night's ride, he was greeted the same morning by the telegram Thomas had sent from Erie, announcing the arrest of Wales. Physically jaded as he was, its contents imparted fresh vigor to his elastic system, and he immediately hastened on to Philadelphia.

It is fair to assume, perhaps, that the Superintendent was highly elated at this important capture, to which his own masterly tactics had so largely contributed. But it was by no means to minister to his personal gratification that he started so promptly for the Quaker City. Like the other Superintendents and myself, he was now conscious that our work had but fairly begun. The criminal we had shadowed so patiently had been deftly ensnared, and was safe in our grasp; but after all he has not the right man, at whose door we could lay the charges of forgery. The appearances rather were, indeed, that his only actual crime was related to the mail robberies, either as principal or accomplice. The real forgers were still at large, and if these went unwhipt of justice, her vindication would be anything but satisfactory.

But as the blotting-paper had revealed Wales, so might Wales discover to us the forgers. In some way or another he had undoubtedly participated in their crimes. Besides that, he was steeped in guilt of another kind, and therefore lacking in stability of purpose. If he could only be induced to make a confession, or even disclose the whereabouts of Dudley, the rest of our work might be accomplished without special difficulty. In all the complications and obscurities of the case, the identity of Dudley had loomed out most conspicuous.

" We must have Dudley, at all events," was now the Superintendent's watchword, " and Wales himself must help us catch him !"

The delicate task of breaking down our captive to this point, was that which Mr. Bangs had now entered upon. Its issue was so vital to our success that he preferred assuming it himself, and at once, to delegating its difficulties in less competent hands. The experienced detective well knew, that even as clay which has been freshly ground and moistened is plastic to the touch of the artist's finger, so the mind of a newly-made prisoner is susceptible to impressions of hope and fear. However hardened to it a criminal may afterwards become, the first privation of liberty is always a terrible blow to him. It seldom fails to weaken even the most resolute heart; and especially is he abased who is not an acknowledged law-breaker, but had secretly wrought out his crimes under the guise of social respectability. The hatred of exposure; the agonizing thought of how friends and relatives would take it; the uncertainty as to what evidence is on hand for his conviction—hoping it may be but little, while fearing that it is everything —all excite in him such perturbation of spirit as generally subserves the aims of justice. Even though remorse, or a sense of personal degradation, does not also enter into the account—for base natures are seldom troubled by these—the prisoner is no longer of the same mental calibre or toughness as before. If he does not relieve himself by a confession, and a purpose to brave all consequences, he will submit, while he detests, to the logic of honester men—he will be ready to clutch and cling to every shadow of compromise, and hesitate at no treason that might offer a chance of impunity. His selfishness and his cowardice, his revenge and his animosities, become so many ministers of the law he has defied. He is fitted, in short, to " break down."

The first step of Mr. Bangs, then, was to hold brief conferences with Thomas and Delaney, so as to be informed of the demeanor of their captive down to the latest moment. He caused them to repeat to him separately, and with greater minuteness, the conversation between Wales and Carrie, overheard in the Revere House. He also made a rigorous inspection of the memorandum-book taken from Wales at the time of his arrest. Thus prepared, he caused his coming to be announced to the prisoner, and at once stepped upstairs to the room wherein he was secluded—now recomposed, and refreshed by an ample meal.

With frank solicitude Mr. Bangs first inquired of him if his personal wants had been attended to ; if he now felt good after his long railroad journey ; and if the detectives had shown due courtesy in the performance of their disagreeable duty ?

Wales was seated in a chair near the stove, with one leg thrown carelessly over the other, and replied to these various questions with ready affirmatives, not untinged with pleasantry.

" This is rather a serious trouble in to which your evil associates have led you," next observed the Superintendent gravely.

" I don't quite see it that way," was the quick response of the prisoner; "I fail to perceive that I am in any such serious trouble, and I have no very bad associates that I am aware of."

"I presume," inquired Mr. Bangs, " that our officers read to you the warrant under which you are arrested ?"

" Mr. Thomas read a warrant to me, sir," replied Wales quite tranquilly; "but I really don't know what to make of it. It charges me with something in which I had neither act nor part, and in fact I don't know of my doing anything against the law except gambling."

Such answers as these were not unexpected by Mr. Bangs, who, however, put some further questions, designed to show his intimacy with the details of the felonies, and how deeply Wales was implicated in them. But the latter without any hesitancy encountered them all in a similar fashion, either by flat denial, or ready-witted evasion.

" Now, Wales," at last said the Superintendent, in a tone of some severity, "this is the merest trifling with my time, and with your own grave situation. You are

here in our custody and power, and we have abundant
proof of your guilt. For months past we have kept
close in your tracks, in Redrock and out of it, and we
know everything that has been going on. The reports
of the detectives who have shadowed you, even to your
least movement, are on file in our office down-stairs.
For all that we desire to be more lenient with you than
with the others—your associates in these daring frauds.
You know them, and the parts they have taken, and it
is your best interest to do what is right by making the
fullest disclosures concerning them. It is the only rep-
aration, too, that you can make for the great crimes
of which you have yourself been guilty."

The prisoner received this admonition in sullen
silence, and affected even a derisive smile at the suggestion that he had been guilty of great crimes. The
expression did not escape the notice of Mr. Bangs, who
continued :

"I assure you it can do no good to deceive yourself
as to the gravity of your crimes, and the heavy penalty
they involve. And aside from such penalty to yourself
you should not forget what their consequences must be
to your respected parents. They neither shared in your
frauds, nor were conscious of their heinous character,
and yet, their hearts must ache, and their home be made
desolate, because of your crime and degradation ; nor
can I well imagine what their feelings must be, when
they now learn that you had become a thief even years

before these occurrences, that their cherished first-born
was piling up disgrace for himself, and misery for them,
when he was a sworn and trusted agent of the national
postal service."

Wales appeared to wince under these terrible blows
but it was not the Superintendent's purpose to crush
out all hope from his bosom.   He continued, in a kindly
way :

" But while I warn you that this last feature of your
career may now be forced to the light, and that the Post-
master-General would fail in his public duty if he did
not take action thereupon, I will not say that it must
necessarily be so, or that he may not be influenced by
the mitigating circumstances in the present case.   To
these mitigating circumstances you can yourself add
the strongest of all.   Suppose, for instance, he were
made aware that you had helped the cause of justice
by surrendering these forgers, he might well be induced
to say to a court or district-attorney : ' The government
cannot ignore this man's acts, but he was formerly a
trusted employee of the department, and through the
evil associations of later days has been led into what he
now seems to deplore ; the department, therefore, is so
far impressed by his repentance, and by other matters
brought to its notice, that it craves for him as lenient a
judgment as the law will permit.'   You have sense
enough to know that an appeal such as this would season

8

justice with mercy, and probably reduce your punish‧ment to a minimum."

A ray, as of the soft light of hope, seemed to struggle through the set desperation that had covered the face of Wales. He listened to the Superintendent with keen re‧gard, but as yet without giving any sign of a relert‧ing purpose.

" And how much better for yourself would this be," added Mr. Bangs, cheerily, " and above all for the poor old couple in Redrock, than as an obstinate, uncon‧fessed criminal to have to expiate your offenses through long years of imprisonment."

In a few striking sentences the Superintendent now pictured to his hearer the calamities which would fall on his parents in the latter dread contingency—their an‧guished loneliness, their clouded home circle, their lin‧gering years of grief and humiliation, and the proba‧bility that they would at last sink into premature graves long ere the prison doors could open to restore their son !

At this point Wales seemed about to interrupt or protest, but the Superintendent was resolved that his mental overthrow should be complete. He quickly re‧sumed :

" But the destinies of your own family are not all that depend on your attitude under this charge. You have a fair young friend in North Adams, whom I shall presume you love, and I ask you to consider how she will feel."

Wales here looked up at the face of Mr. Bangs with such an anxious and beseeching scrutiny that the Superintendent, in spite of himself, paused a brief moment.

"I ask you," he resumed, "how she will feel when your obstinate silence has dragged her from the merciful retirement of home, and forced her on the witness-stand of a criminal court to tell what she knows of yourself and your associates in crime."

As he spoke these words Mr. Bangs looked full in the eyes of Wales. For a time the latter quailed not, but at length he changed color, and his glance fell cowering beneath the gaze of the Superintendent, who now followed up his advantage.

"Yes, sir," he continued with energy, "if you yourself do not tear away the secrecy that surrounds these forgers, Carrie Levison will undoubtedly be forced to do it. And what she must reveal during that process, as you well know, may strike harder and deeper than even the most vindictive prosecution could desire. Alone and conspicuous in a crowded court-room, agitated by her surroundings and badgered by some relentless lawyer, she cannot but heap destruction on the very head she would screen. She will tell all, Wales, *all*—and I need not inform *you* what that comprises. And what, pray, will be the consequences to herself ? What will be her next step ? She would leave such a court-room a forlorn and branded girl—one who had not only looked the prison doors on the man she loved, but forever closed against herself the portals of society! Is it too much to apprehend that in such dire straits she would hasten to the nearest drug-store, or to some steep river bank—and then, then—you know the rest; discovery of a young girl's corpse, a gaping crowd, a coroner's inquest, and lastly, a brief, chilling verdict to record the close of a sad life-history."

Wales had covered up his face with his hands toward the conclusion of these startling utterances. The Superintendent felt that he might now leave him to his reflections—that the seed he had flung out had not fallen among rocks. He concluded gently:

"I have said nothing whatever to you, Wales, of the genuine manliness there is in acknowledging one's offenses and exhibiting proper regret for them; nor of fifty other points that I think of in this connection. Many of these will occur to your own mind. You are a young man, gifted with some energy and talents, and may yet carve a bright future for yourself, if you do not blast the prospect by defying an upright public sentiment. You did not ask, and do not seem to relish, my advice in this matter; but I have fairly shown you the brighter view of your case, although not all the darker. If I find time within a day or two, I will call in again to hear from you."

The prisoner sat motionless, silent, stricken.

The superintendent then retired from the room; the officer whose turn it was to keep guard over Wales re-entering without a moment's delay.

———◆———

CHAPTER XXI.

Mr. Bangs succeeds in securing a Confession from Wales.—
Some of the Plunder is also Recovered.

THE interview just recorded took place on Saturday afternoon. During the remainder of the evening, and throughout the following day, Wales continued in a kind of gloomy lethargy. He was apparently revolving in his own mind the suggestions of Mr. Bangs, and painting to himself, perhaps, in still more somber colors, the consequences of his conviction to those near and dear to him. Occasionally he rallied for a moment and made some remark to Thomas or other detectives, who relieved the latter at stated intervals. In no instance did such remarks apply to himself or his case, but always to indifferent or frivolous subjects, as if they were so many efforts to escape from a distasteful self-communion. Acting under instructions, however, the detectives gave him no excuse for a sustained conversation; but read or smoked in silence, and responded to his questions or observations only with frigid monosyllables. This threw Wales entirely back upon himself, and left him no other alternative but to meditate on his situation, present and prospective.

Mr. Bangs, of course, heard from time to time of how his prisoner was occupied; and felt no desire to break in on the current of his reflections. Sufficient had been said, he thought, to give ample room and verge enough for a review by Wales of his own sad predicament; and to lead him out logically to the conclusion desired—that a full confession was the best for his own interests. Late Sunday evening the Superintendent called into the room, and after inquiring as to the captive's health, exchanged a few remarks with him about the weather, and other such commonplaces. The share of Wales in this brief conversation was clearly that of a person who was preoccupied by graver themes; and who suffered the abasement which crime ever feels in the presence of rectitude. Of himself or his concerns he spoke not a word. He had evidently not yet screwed up his courage to the sticking-point; which in his case meant the plowing up of the past and its criminal associations, to prepare for the growth of a more manly future. Mr. Bangs, therefore, who is a true Lavater in his profession, remained with Wales but a few brief moments. As he returned down stairs he said to himself: "We must give him enough time—the medicine works well!"

Monday passed over without any incident worth mention—gloomily enough for the captive Wales;

brimful of occupation for the busy Superintendent. The latter did not quite forget his prisoner, however; he merely left him alone—"in order," as Mr. Thomas pertinently remarked, "that he might work out his own salvation."

The following day, about noon, the officer named was seated in the room with Wales, when the latter jumped up from his chair, and without any preamble inquired if Mr. Bangs was in the building?

"Can't say," replied Thomas, without even looking up from the book which he had been reading for an hour or so previous.

The prisoner sighed heavily, and without speaking any further, made a few hasty turns up and down the room. In stolen glances Mr. Thomas noted—that he had his hands thrust firmly into his pants pockets; that he was really walking, and not, as usual, lounging; and that the dark corrugations of his brow had given place to a more tranquil but resolute expression.

"He's going to break, I bet five dollars on it!" was the mental proposition of the detective to some imaginary sceptic.

"Did you want to see the Superintendent?" he next inquired of Wales, aloud.

"Yes, please; I should like to see him to-day," replied the captive, returning to his chair near the stove.

Thomas at once passed the word outside, but it was quite half an hour before Mr. Bangs entered the room, and temporarily released the detective from his charge. He greeted Wales courteously, and took a chair in front of that which the latter occupied. A single glance at the face of the prisoner informed him that his success had been complete—more so than he had dared to expect; for whereas he might have been content with the betrayal of the forgers, he now saw plainly that Wales intended to make a "clean breast" of it. There was no mistaking the quiet purpose of the eye, averted partially though it was; nor the frank resignation on his features, paler even than usual, but freed from the rough lines of suspense and obstinacy. The swindler had become a man again, in having resolved on the purgation of his conscience. It were needless to detail the long interview that ensued between Wales and my General Superintendent. The criminal confessed with absolute unreserve; and Mr. Bangs had little more to do than to name the points on which he desired to be enlightened.

Almost at the outset came the explanation of the secret that had baffled and perplexed us from the beginning of the operations—that in all the thieving, swindling and forging transactions there were but two accomplices, W. R. Wales himself, and R. L. Dudley! The former, in person, was the one who had plundered the mails; and the latter had been the forger and collector of the drafts, first at Pittsburg under his real name, and elsewhere under the various aliases of Randall, Cone, Davis, Rugby, and Gray.

With regard to their methods Mr. Bangs elicited, that having himself been in the mail service on the Yarmouth and Cleveland line, Wales had become acquainted with the different route agents, and when traveling over the road could at all times ride in the mail cars. It was his frequent custom, also, to take a hand on such occasions in the distribution of the mails; either to lighten the general labors, or to accommodate individual indolence. In Hobart's car he was specially welcome; not only because of his early intimacy with that individual, but because he usually brought with him good cigars and a flask of brandy or whisky, and Hobart was a person who relished a sly stimulant. Occasionally, indeed, he used the stimulant so freely, that it promoted the very indolence which made the thief's opportunity. Once engaged in sorting the letters, the latter was enabled to pick out such as were likely to contain money or drafts, unaided and undetected by any one in the mail car.

Meanwhile Dudley would have established himself under a pretense of business in some eastern city, where the drafts of a suitable character would be brought to him by the thief for forgery and collection. When this was accomplished, an equal division of the plunder ensued, and Wales then returned to Redrock until Dudley was again ready for him. This, of course, would be as soon as he was sufficiently known in some other community, and under a different name, to procure

8*

identification at the express offices. Then, a fresh trip on the railroad from Yarmouth along to Buffalo, a visit to old friends in the mail car, whisky and cigars for such silly-pates as Hobart, and another bunch of stolen money letters, renewed and continued the infamous programme. The operations in which the two criminals had been engaged included every one of those reported to the Agency, and the total of their plunder was nearly thirty thousand dollars!

Of Dudley Mr. Bangs now learned, that during the period under consideration he had no settled place of abode. He had always traveled with his wife, and very rarely resided in the city where he established his bogus business—preferring some quiet village within easy railroad access. Of the present whereabouts of the forger, Wales could only say, that when they last separated, which was in the city of New York, Dudley informed him that he would make his home for a time at Monroe, Michigan. His intention then was, to prepare for a new campaign of fraud at Detroit, although Wales had told him that for his own part he was sick of the dangerous game, and proposed to settle down on the plunder then in hand. It was probable that the exact address of Dudley would ere long become known, through his writing to Cleveland or Yarmouth, to advise Wales where he should bring more stolen drafts.

Mrs. Dudley, the prisoner affirmed, was quite aware of her husband's criminal transactions, and mostly carried his money; while her unmarried sister at Pittsburg knew there was something wrong, but certainly not its exact nature. Meanwhile, excepting this latter person,—Miss Lizzie Green eaf,—who maintained with the Dudleys a semi-occasional correspondence, he knew of no living being who would have their address. Of this young lady, Wales spoke in the highest terms, both as to her personal probity and stainless character. Naturally she was much devoted to her sister, and however criminal might be that sister's husband, would not willingly be the instrument of his capture.

Concerning his young paramour, Miss Carrie Levison, Wales was fain to admit that she knew there was an illicit confederacy between himself and Bradley; but he was so reluctant to tell the precise extent of her knowledge, and exhibited such genuine anguish at the idea of incriminating her, that the Superintendent mercifully forebore to press him on this point.

"For the present at least," thought Mr. Bangs, "we may leave the poor thing in her seclusion,—nor ever disturb her, perhaps, if we can reach Mr. Dudley by other means."

To anticipate the risk that Wales was playing him false, the Superintendent asked him if he would consent to abide at the Agency until we accomplished Dudley's arrest,—or, would he prefer to be formally charged at the Police Court, and committed to Moyamensing Prison?

Convinced, as the captive was, that his best chance lay in Dudley being arrested through his confession, and indicted before himself, he pleaded earnestly to be allowed to remain where he was. He would employ the interval, he said, in making what restitution he could, by yielding up the plunder in his possession, and facilitating by his disclosures the capture of the other criminal. As an earnest of his good intentions he at once gave a very full description of Dudley and wife, as also of such of his belongings as might serve to track them down.

As a preliminary to the new search in which we must now engage, Mr. Bangs communicated to the Post Office authorities at Washington the account of our success thus far, and the use that was being made of Wales for the capture of the more guilty forger. As it was abundantly clear that publicity would defeat this search, and defraud Dame Justice of her rights against Dudley, the Department, under the advice of the Attorney General, consented to our having custody of Wales, so long as he would himself agree to remain at the Agency. If at any time before the arrest of Dudley he should claim his right to be sent to the public prison, he was to be accommodated without delay !

But Wales was in no hurry to change. He wrote to his brother at Redrock, explaining that he had entered into an oil speculation in Pennsylvania, and would be away from home for a limited period.

His money and other valuables were now taken from him, and held for Adams' Express Company pending his trial. In their favor also, a check was obtained from him for the money he held in the bank at Yarmouth and he surrendered to them the deed of the quarry property at Redrock, which represented all of his plunder that remained.

CHAPTER XXII.

Wales, having Confessed, is further Relieved by giving a History of Himself, his Accomplices, the still uncaught Dudley, and of their Acquaintance, Experiences and Depredations.

ONCE having disclosed the true character and extent of his misdeeds, Wales seemed to experience a certain kind of cheerfulness. From being morose and taciturn, he now became social and communicative. Other men in his position might have sunk their own thoughts and anxieties in the perusal of books and newspapers, of which a plentiful supply was ever within his reach. But Wales was not the kind of a man to find comfort in reading of any kind. Human companionship and conversation were the necessities of his nature, and he would frequently spend hours at a stretch discoursing with his watchful custodians.

As might be presumed of a person with his shallow and conceited mind, these confabulations referred chiefly to himself. His own impudent crimes he still seemed to regard as so many creditable exploits; and on the slenderest encouragement he would recount them in every detail with the most complacent gusto.

This circumstance may throw grave doubts on the merits of his confession to Mr. Bangs, and on the purpose of genuine reform which would be its proper sequence. But my duty is to present the man as he really was, and not to set him up as a type of repentance, and as a criminal who impressed myself as the very incarnation of duplicity and selfishness.

Although the captive told enough to Mr. Bangs to give consistency to our estimate of Dudley, much was still learned of the twain that possessed for us a lively interest. From these intermittent revelations, sometimes made to one detective and sometimes to another, I gathered a more connected history of the rogues and their iniquitous partnership, which may fittingly be related between the capture of the one and the further pursuit of the other.

Wales was a native of the Buckeye State, and first saw the light in Sandusky county, about twenty-seven years before the opening of this narrative. At that time, and during much of his boyhood, his father kept a wagon and blacksmith shop, and usually farmed a small tract of land. As a pioneer craftsman in a new country, he thus made a plentiful subsistence for his wife and young children; and life was as gladsome with them as the days were long. The strokes of his hammer on the chiming anvil, and of his axe on the tough young tree-stocks, made music delectable in the ears of a contented wife. The gambols of his children in the clearing, and the ring of their young voices on the way from the log-built school-house, were the sights and sounds that made pleasurable a father's toil.

Well had it been for the family, indeed—parents and children alike—if no larger sphere and more ambitious pursuits had ever seduced them from this simple life. It were, at least, fair to presume that the blacksmith's first-born son had never then been hunted as a felon through the land.

It was while the latter was yet in pinafores that his father contracted a taste which but very rarely subserves the well-being of its possessor. I have chosen to call it a taste, but it might better be branded as a disease ; and some there are who claim that it is purely an American one—just like the dyspepsia, for instance. At all events a very appropriate name for it would be that of " office fever ;" its most prominent and distressing symptom being an unquenchable thirst for public dignities. The elder Wales was first attacked by it as a pathmaster and school trustee, then as a town clerk, next as a postmaster, and so from one function to another, away up the ladder of little brief authority, until at last it had become chronic and incurable. Thus it was that we found him at Redrock as mayor and justice of the peace.

Now, as many of these successive preferments involved a change of domicile, it had come to pass in time that farming and blacksmithing and wagon-making fell back to a very minor place in the affections of the rising settler. He continued to be abundantly prosperous, it is true, but his earnings were no longer bedewed and hallowed by the sweat of positive labor. He removed from one locality to another in the northern part of the State, until none could be truly regarded as home, while the boys, who should have stood by to take axe and sledge from his stiffening hands, were sprouting into a sapless and dawdling manhood. Assuredly it was not to be expected that the sons of the village mayor and justice—the maker and unmaker of the district Congressman—should toil in a grimy leather apron at the dingy forge hearth, or blister their white fingers on a vulgar plow-handle. No, of course not; they, too, must have office; they, too, must be nourished on public pap; and while waiting around loose for the appointments to come, they must play cards and billiards, and visit the big cities, and debauch themselves generally by what simpletons call "seeing life."

It was from such graduation as this, that shortly after his majority William R. Wales was made a postal route-agent, on the line running eastward through Yarmouth and Cleveland. About two or three months subsequently Hobart was appointed on the same car with him, and for a considerable time both continued to work at the same table. A similarity of tastes—and some of them, be it said, were grossly vicious—soon led to the formation of a close intimacy, though Wales denied to us persistently that he ever saw any reason to conclude that Hobart was dishonest.

He was not very long, however, in becoming a thief himself. The expensive vices of the cities, and an almost barbaric taste for trinkets, could not well be indulged in on the meager salary of a postal clerk. The greenbacks were fresh and crisp in those days, and he soon learned to distinguish the letters that contained them. So was it with bank bills, and other money enclosures, large numbers of which he appropriated without scruple and spent without remorse.

At that period he could not make any use of drafts ; and was even so ignorant of business methods as scarcely to know their pecuniary significance. When he happened to violate a letter containing one of those instruments, or an equally inconvertible money order, he would destroy it by fire on the first opportunity, lest accident should reveal and make it an agent in his destruction.

Although clouded by suspicion, and occasionally watched and baited by the Special Agents,—as we have heard him vaunting to Miss Levison at the Revere House,—Wales succeeded throughout in escaping detection; nor did he leave the service of the Post Office until a change of administration caused the usual dislodgment of *patriots* all over the land.

Although now married to an estimable young wife, the career of the discharged postal-clerk became one of restlessness and vicissitude. For a while he kept a restaurant in Cleveland: then a fruit and game stand in Yarmouth; and again traveled as sales agent for a firm of Toledo manufacturers. From the last named city he removed to New York, where in rapid succession he held and abandoned two or three fair mercantile situations. In short, he was many things by turns, and nothing long.

Once more he turned his face to the great West, but nowhere could settle down to habits of patient industry. Vain, vicious and inconstant, wherever he went his sins appeared to find him out. The man who had become a thief,—though undiscovered,—and a libertine,—though cloaked,—was scarcely the one to clamber up the steeps of self-denial to success.

What his conjugal life may have been during this period can only be imagined from the resulting facts. With the last ramparts of honor and principle fast crumbling away, it is reasonable to infer that the sanctities of a pure love had become quite as unpalatable to him as a life of honest labor. Well has it been said of the first steps in guilt, that

> "They hang upon a precipice
> Whose steep descent in last perdition ends."

At all events, somewhat more than a year before the point at which our story opens, Wales had abandoned his loyal wife and drifted to the city of St. Louis, with the avowed determination to rid himself of her entirely.

At this time Wales was in possession of about four hundred dollars in money, and he lounged for a while about the "Great City of the Future," without any settled purpose, or any very strenuous effort to obtain employment. On first arriving in the city he had rented a small lodging room in a private house; but after some little time the landlady suggested to him that he might have better accommodations at a reduced rate, if he would take one of her large rooms, and agree to share its accommodations with some other lodger.

"Really I have no objection, Mrs. Burroughs, so long as the party is a gentleman," was the response of Wales to the lady's proposition, caressing as he spoke his amber mustache, so as to display to advantage the Alaska diamond that newly glittered on his finger.

"You need not receive any one, sir, who is not a gentleman," rejoined the landlady with professional dignity. "So long as you remain at my house you are unlikely to meet persons of any other class."

On this assurance the hair-brained exquisite condescended to be satisfied, and the transition to the larger room was duly accomplished.

About a week subsequently Wales entered his room one evening to find it occupied by a strange man, whom he rightly conjectured to be his future fellow-lodger.

The latter was a well-dressed individual, of engaging presence, and dignified, gentlemanly deportment, somewhat taller, and a few years older, than Wales himself.

With a faint trace, or affectation, more likely—of English accent, he apologized for his intrusion, and explained the circumstances under which the landlady had sent him there. He did it, withal, in such well-chosen language, and with such stately grace, that Wales was completely charmed with him. He acknowledged to himself that he could not have desired a nicer roommate, and at once made up his mind that Mrs. Burroughs was an excellent judge of gentlemen.

A proper understanding having been arrived at in regard to the room, its new occupant introduced himself as Robert L. Dudley, late of Pittsburg; Wales reciprocated by the disclosure of his own name; and in a very brief while the two were chatting of their views and experiences like friends of long years' standing.

CHAPTER XXIII.

A Continuance of Wales' Confession.

THE companion whom fate had assigned to Wales was indeed an engaging personage. His conversation, at will, betokened an educated intellect and familiarity with good society, as well as large experience in the ways of the world. As a business man, he appeared to be one who might have made a fortune at almost anything; and socially he was competent to win friends wherever he desired.

Notwithstanding these advantages, inherent and acquired, Dudley was a man who had really neither money nor friends. If Wales was the abnormal and tainted offshoot of one condition of society, the Englishman was a noxious and weedy outgrowth of another and an older one. The former despised work as his father became an office-holder; the latter had never learned to work, because, forsooth, his father was a " gentleman !" Neither one nor the other could recognize any dignity whatever in labor; and as a necessary consequence, each had " lost his grip " on the stanchions of right principle.

The son of the western place-hunter, and the scion of blue-blooded gentility,—for Dudley laid claim to a kinship with " the best families,"—had met on the same level as drones and leeches of society. They had reached it by different routes, but the impulses which had led them together were the same.

Dudley was not long in gaining an influence over his less crafty companion. On this very first night of their intercourse he ascertained that Wales was not in-any business, and little cared indeed, what kind of busi-ness he should undertake, so long as there was " money to be made in it."

" Are you engaged in anything yourself, Mr. Dud-ley ?" inquired the ex-mail agent, as the conversation proceeded.

" Haw ! my dear fellah, you never catch Bob Dud-ley without a finger in some kind of pie. Yes, sir ; I've just come on now from Porkopolis, where I spent a few days fixing up a little picture on which I think there's a devilish good stake to be made."

" A picture !" exclaimed Wales, incredulously, for he was well-informed in all the dodges of novelty dealers ; " there's not much to be made now-a-days on pictures or books."

" I know it," answered the newcomer, promptly ; " but you don't suppose, Mr. Wales, that I'm such a noodle as to go around like a sixpenny peddler trying to sell pictures. No, by George, sir ; I can do considerably better than that, and without much exertion either."

Dudley had now an attentive listener, and explained that his visit to Cincinnati had been made for the purpose of getting up a picture of the proposed new fountain

and its surroundings. From the artists' dainty design
a photographer had made for him several large copies,
and he intended, both in St. Louis and Cincinnati, to
canvas for business advertisements to be arranged around
them—the same to be charged for at a goodly figure.
He would then place his pictures in elegant frames, and
put one of them in the main saloon of each of the six
propellers that plied between Cincinnati, St. Louis, and
New Orleans ; obtaining first, of course, the permission
of the captains.

The speculator here unfolded a large roll of card-
board, and displayed to his admiring friend a copy of
the fountain picture, on whose artistic excellences he
made a florid eulogium. On this particular point
Wales was not much of a judge, so he readily acqui-
esced in the criticisms of his well-bred friend.

The latter then took from his pocket a neat silver
extension-rule, and measured off for the edification of
Wales the marginal space which he hoped to cover
with paying business cards. So many inches long by
so many inches wide were to constitute a standard
square ; and so many standard squares at so many dollars each, represented the handsome amount to be derived from the advertisers ;—the only outlay being for
the printing and frames. It was a simple arithmetical
fact, claimed Dudley, that after paying so much for
printing, and so much to the frame maker, so many
hundred dollars must remain to the worker of the

scheme. As soon as the first set of pictures were sufficiently known and admired, too, a further supply of copies could be obtained, and a new class of advertisers might be approached, who would prefer to have their cards displayed in the hotel reading-rooms. Thus could the enterprise be profitably extended in various directions.

"But will the advertisers bite?" inquired the still mistrustful Wales.

"Bite? Of course they'll bite, sir," was the ready answer. "Why, there's such enthusiasm in Cincinnati just now on the subject of this very fountain, that I'm convinced the best firms in the city will run after these squares, and snap them up like hot cakes."

"Perhaps they won't be allowed on board the propellers, Mr. Dudley?"

"Hindeed, won't they?" returned that gentleman, "W'ere's the river captain that won't be delighted to have it?—a choice specimen of art—an adornment to the saloon—an evidence of taste in the Queen City of the West—and all that kind of stuff? W'y, there's none of 'em can afford to be without it, sir!"

"But the doose of it all is, my dear fellah," resumed Dudley with a sigh, "that I've scarely enough blunt to carry the affair through. I thought to write to fawther—who is now in London—but 'e's 'eard not long since of my having married a Pittsburg girl, and I don't expect a thing, dem it, but to get cut off with a shilling. The governor cawnt even tolerate the idea that we should marry out of our own set."

This was the very kind of bombast to impose on the witless Wales.

"Couldn't the thing be pushed out on a credit, Mr. Dudley?" he now inquired—the speculative instincts of the West being strong within him.

"I have though of that," answered Dudley; "that I might be able to stave off the printer and frame maker until the advertisers came down with the dust- But in that way, you know, I should be giving up the best of the profits; while if I could pay the confounded fellahs right off, the work could be done for about half the figure, you know."

"What do you say now, Wales," he resumed, "to going in with me on this picture and taking half profits? If you've got a little rhino to invest, we can make a good thing of it in a few days; besides having a pleasant trip to see the lassies st Porkopolis. Working on it together, you know, we can soon pick up the advertisements, and get the returns in speedily as well."

With very little further importunity, Wales agreed to this proposition, and even informed Dudley of the extent of his financial wealth, so entirely was he fascinated by the specious Briton.

Next morning the new partners went down to the levee to visit such of the propellers as were there, or

9

might make a landing. Within two or three days they had obtained permission from all their captains to hang the fountain picture in the saloons, such permission being reduced to writing and signed, so as to satisfy intending advertisers that their cards would not fail to have the promised display. They next started around town to canvas for advertisements to fill the margin spaces, Wales becoming hourly more devoted to his patrician friend.

But the latter part of the programme was rather more difficult than the newly-made associates had reckoned on. The business outlook of the season was far from being a bright one, and the larger number of St. Louis merchants were much more disposed to curtail expenses than to hazard their surplus in advertisements.

The demand for "standard squares" was accordingly very limited, and Wales and Dudley,—who were both cut out for sybarites rather than drudges,—found their promised "walk over" a decidedly up-hill tramp.

While thus wearily engaged they were informed in the city that other parties were canvassing, in a sluggish kind of way, for advertisements to be published on a play-bill sheet. This was to be used as the official programme at Rankin's and De Bar's theaters, and a little French music-seller named Bartel was stated to be the person who controlled the project.

"Why don't you take up that play-bill?" said the

printer one day to Wales, who had called to have a solitary advertisement put in type.

" How ?   Do you think there's anything in it ? "

" You just bet there is," said the tradesman. " Bartel could make a good thing on it if he would only devote to it the necessary time. I tell you there's a blamed sight more money in it than in your Cincinnati picture."

" How do you make that out ? " returned Wales, who still believed there was a gold mine somewhere in Dudley's scheme ; or, at all events, that Cincinnati would compensate them for the apathy of St. Louis.

" Well, you're a fool if you can't see it," rejoined the man of types. " For the one who would read a business card round a picture on a steamboat, there are scores who will scan every line on a play-bill in the theater, and city advertisers know that right well."

On this information the associates decided to abandon the fountain picture, and at once bought out for a consideration Mr. Bartel's interest in the play-bill, the same to be paid by installments after the issue of the sheet. To carry out this undertaking they then arranged a more formal partnership, under the style and title of "H. Norman & Co.," Wales being Mr. Harry Norman and Dudley the " Co." As the former confessed to his now cherished associate, he employed such an alias so that his wife should not learn of his whereabouts.

In this new adventure a larger measure of success attended them. A brief but energetic canvas resulted in bringing a fair share of patronage to the play-bill, and the sheet bid fair to become a recognized advertising medium. But the installments due to the Frenchman were meanwhile looming up for payment, and for a time, at least, would absorb the best part of its income. This didn't exactly suit "Norman & Co.," who, on the approach of the first pay-day, collected on every hand as much money as possible, and without as much as say ing "good-by," either to the printer or Mr. Bartel, absconded from St. Louis and hastened up stream into Ohio.

Arrived at Cincinnati, or Porkopolis, as the high toned Dudley usually called it, the confederates made a pause to survey the situation. By this time they had come to understand each other well. There was no occasion for either to assume the mask of honesty with the other, and so, without disguise or hesitancy, they fell to mapping out schemes of plunder, as others might lay plans for legitimate undertakings.

In the course of one of their conversations Wales now mentioned the fact that he was formerly a postal-clerk on the Eastern mail route through Ohio; and also recounted some of his exploits as a mail depredator. Although despising his friend's braggadocio, Dudley on this occasion endured it in patience, and heard every detail with a devilish intensity of interest.

"Are you still acquainted on the road ?" he inquired of Wales, during a pause in the shameless recital.

"Oh! certainly," answered the Ohioan; "I have lots of friends there; I could ride in the mail car with the boys any time I have a mind to."

"By Jove, my dear fellah, that's just the thing," exclaimed Dudley; "wait a minute."

After an interval of reflection the knave proceeded to outline his felonious plans, winding up with the assurance that if Wales could get hold of letters with commercial drafts in them, he, Dudley, would undertake to "doctor them up," and get the money on them, —which they would then divide equally as partners in the risk.

"Why, I have often burned the darned things in the stove," observed Wales, dejectedly, "not knowing how to make anything out of them."

"Well, *you* might not know, Mr. Wales," returned Dudley, with an air of tart superiority, "but *I* know the way very well. I have cooked and realized on bogus drafts many a time; so that if I could only handle a few genuine ones I would squeeze the money out of them without any danger whatever. I could collect on them, sir, just as *you* might on so many bank notes."

It was not in the disposition of Dudley to be very open-mouthed about his own transgressions, but at this point it seemed necessary to impress Wales with his capacity for the work of fraud. The latter was not long in yielding to the superior rogue. He consented to "go in" with Dudley as a partner in the infamous work,—he to steal drafts; Dudley to forge and collect them.

Having thus arranged things to his satisfaction, the forger at once started by way of Pittsburg for Buffalo; and Wales took train for Kelvin, Ohio, where he could strike the Eastern mail so as to reach the same city.

The Mansion House in Buffalo was agreed upon as the place of rendezvous.

--------◆--------

CHAPTER XXIV.

Additional Exploits of the two Criminals, as related by Wales to Mr. Pinkerton's officers.

WHEN Wales touched the line of the Michigan Southern Railroad at Kelvin, he had still three or four hours to wait for the arrival of the eastward-bound mail train. His design was to take passage by the same; travel in the postal car in Hobart's company; continue with the train until its arrival at Buffalo; and trust to the heedlessness or stupidity of the thirsty mail clerk, for the opportunities to embezzle some draft letters. Only too well had he learned how to distinguish the appearance of letters containing either money or drafts.

After partaking of a meal at the restaurant he strolled out through the little village to smoke a cigar. The air was hushed and pensive as if pregnant with coming storms. The sun was fast sinking in the West, and the sky in that quarter was piled up with massy clouds which took a glaring and portentous light from his parting beams. A something there was in the whole aspect of nature, significant of man's littleness, and prompting him to self-abasement in the presence of Omnipotence.

As the glance of the intending thief wandered involuntarily among the flame-tipped clouds, he was carried back in fancy to his sinless childhood. Thus had he often beheld them, out beyond the forest that encircled the old forge, and the log school-house, and the pleasant home of his early days. But as he well remembered, they held no threat or omen for him then Suggestive only of wonder and admiration, in boyish hyperbole he had hailed them as "God's Mountains."

But now, alas! how different. There was a frown of rebuke in every somber cloud-chasm; a flash of anger in every burning cloud-crest, for, " thus conscience does make cowards of us all."

Wales was not exactly superstitious, but his reflections of this evening were gloomy in the extreme. Only as a dim and feeble little ray, did the light of a better purpose come to him. Nevertheless, it was clearly discernible, for no man is tempted beyond the strength of

man's resolve. Only those who *will* fall, really *do* fall.
Even still there was time enough to step back from
the precipice of crime. Even now he could tear himself from the malign influence of Dudley, and build up
a new life where the tempter could not reach him.
Even yet he might disinfect his nature, and renovate
his heart, so as again to become worthy of a wife's and
mother's caresses.

But how was all this to be accomplished ? what must
he do to be socially saved ?

Wales was far too intelligent a man not to perceive
the true answer to his difficulties. All the processes of
nature, and all the triumphs of humanity, proclaimed
the medicines for his disease.

They were Labor and Moderation; he must toil, and
he must deny himself.

As he now realized the universal mandate, the
nerveless craven fell prone and helpless back into
his temptation. He would not toil, and he would
not deny himself. His wayward disposition, and
his acquired habits, had entirely indisposed him to
sacrifice of any kind. In short, he was a ready-made
criminal, and just the kind of instrument that Dudley
wanted.

About seven o'clock in the evening, the mail train
from the west came thundering along to the depot at
Kelvin. Before re-entering the station Wales had procured some nice cigars and a bottle of whisky, and

with these in his valise he now passed at once into the mail car. Hobart received him with the old-time cordiality; and as the night wore on, and the parching dust found lodgment in his throat, he hesitated not to partake of the liquor which his former comrade pressed on him.

It is unnecessary to watch more closely the maneuvers of the mail thief. He "assisted" Clerk Hobart in assorting and making up his letter packages; and when he joined Dudley on the morrow at the Mansion House in Buffalo, he had with him quite a number of pilfered draft letters.

Not wishing to incur any risks at Buffalo, the swindlers at once took train for Albany in the same State. Assuming there the name of C. H. Rugby, Dudley forged the indorsements on three of the drafts, and put them for collection into the office of the American Express Company.

The fate of these drafts the reader has learned in a former chapter. They were the same of which the proceeds were returned to New York by a scrupulous express agent, and which Dudley entirely failed to collect through the wise precaution of the eminent old dry-goods merchant, H. B. Claflin. The letter of introduction which was presented on that occasion was a clever forgery, the writing being imitated from the genuine communication of a customer in Kansas City, found among the letters rifled by Wales.

When the alarmed and disappointed forger left Mr. Claflin's store, Wales was waiting for him in a beer saloon on Greenwich street. On hearing of the narrow escape of his accomplice, he became quite solicitous about their further safety; and almost without discussion both concluded that New York was becoming rather warm to hold them. They accordingly crossed over at once to Jersey City, and hastened by the afternoon train to Philadelphia.

The unabashed Dudley was not yet at the limit of his resources. There were still three drafts in his possession; one of which, for about $1,200, was drawn on a New York bank. From the Quaker City the swindler telegraphed next morning to the cashier of that institution, to inquire if the draft was good and negotiable. His dispatch was so framed as to intimate that it had been indorsed to him, but that he was shy of receiving it because it was eight days old.

The telegraph reply of the bank being satisfactory, he promptly forged the name of the payee, and by a fresh indorsement made the draft payable to the order of Flynn Brothers, Norwalk, Ohio.

As Mr. Malachy Flynn of Norwalk, Dudley now called at a wholesale grocery house on Front street, where he purchased about $750 worth of merchandise for shipment to the pretended firm. In settlement of this invoice he gave the twelve-hundred-dollar draft, and received for the residue the check of the confiding grocer for $450—that merchant congratulating himself, no doubt, that his house was at length snatching the Ohio trade from the rival emporiums of New York. The patronizing Mr. Flynn, before leaving, "tasted" some of the grocer's ripe Madeira; directed the making up of a package of samples; promised a fresh order by an early mail; and gave minute and thoughtful instructions about the proper shipment of his goods. Then he rejoined Wales in a near-by restaurant.

On hearing his friend's story the latter was jubilant. His rash plunge into felony was not all for naught. They were at last in command of a legitimate money instrument. Together the swindlers now proceeded to a clothing store on Arch street, where Dudley bought a full suit of clothes, and Wales a light Spring overcoat—in payment for which articles the former made a confident tender of the grocer's check.

Now the clothier—being a lineal off-shoot of the house of Israel—had all the wary business instincts of his race; and so, having examined the paper from every possible point of view, he observed:

"Mistair Vlinn, I am sorry—but I haf not de pleasure to recognishe de sheck of de firm on Front sthreet."

"Oh! it's all right, perfectly right, Mr. Daniels," rejoined Dudley, with his usual easy effrontery; "I've just taken the check as change of my own draft, in buying a bill of goods; they hadn't enough legal tender to make the amount, you know. Send it over to the paying bank and you will find it is all right."

An office boy was thereupon sent out to the bank on which the check was drawn, and the instrument being recognized by the teller as that of a customer with a portly balance, was at once pronounced to be " good."

" But I muss haf it shertified," persisted the cautious Hebrew, even when the boy had brought back the reassuring answer.

Once more the messenger was dispatched to the bank, and this time Dudley made an excuse to follow him out, having a vague apprehension of some impending disaster. Unfortunately for the grocer, however, his bankers were only too ready to do honor to his signature, and immediately certified and sent back the check.

Without further ado the balance in greenbacks was then counted out to Dudley, and before two hours had elapsed the swindlers were riding westward on the Pennsylvania Railroad.

Wales was now completely in the toils. His share of the plunder just obtained was only a trifle over $200,—but this was at least a respite from the dreaded necessity of work, and according to his purview, was thus compensation for all shame and wrong. Besides, he had learned to have a fatal reliance on the fertility of Dudley's cunning. What though the plans of the forger had miscarried at Albany, and placed them for a time in serious jeopardy—had he not promptly perceived it, and wriggled out in safety, and even as he went made a clever grab for the spoils?

"Oh! yes," thought the mail thief to himself, "so long as I work with Dud. there's piles of money in it. He's just the kind o' rooster to put a job through."

With this sort of material to work upon, it was an easy matter for Dudley to persuade his human cat's-paw to call on him in Pittsburg about the 30th of the same month,—undertaking to steal some draft letters on the journey.

"I only missed at Albany," asserted the forger, "through the confounded nicety of that express agent about the identification. In Pittsburg I am well known, however, and can easily get identified for as high as $10,000."

In due time Wales made his appearance in Pittsburg, having again taken a night ride with Hobert, and purloined more letters. It was now and here that he first saw Mrs. Dudley and her unmarried sister,—being privileged, as Mr. Harry Norman, to escort the ladies to some local entertainments.

Under his own proper name, as we have already seen, Dudley succeeded here in making his first collections on forged paper through the medium of the Adams' Express Company. The partition of this plunder gave each of the confederates a sum of $750; which was about the largest amount of money of which Wales had ever had control at one time.

It wrought him but little good. The last vestiges of decency were now cast under foot. Slothful ease and vicious indulgence had been purchased at the cost of a conscience. With these at his beck and call he seemed to have discovered a world to himself. Vain as Malvolio in the play, he could not resist the desire to flaunt his plumage at Redrock. The possession of money would serve not only to cloak his vices, but suggest the belief that he had passed his time in legitimate effort. Before long he would get more of it, too ; and some day or other, perhaps, make a sufficient " haul " to warrant him in retreating into rectitude. This last is a delusion which is rarely wanting in those who have entangled themselves in the mesh of crime.

On his return to the village the thief was met by the announcement that his long-enduring wife had obtained a legal divorce. Besides the fact of his desertion, there had not been wanting proofs that he was a disloyal husband. He was received at his parents' home, however, as one of whom good things might yet be expected. Did ever yet a mother cease to have hope in her first-born ?

But it was a very slender thread on which this mother hung her hopes. Wales had become a willful, self-approved thief ; and held himself in readiness to obey the behests of Dudley.

CHAPTER XXV.

The Chronicles of the Felonious Pair brought down to a Point where the much-desired Dudley became Invisible.

IT was not very long before the summons of Dudley came to his associate at Redrock. The forger sent word that under the name of R. D. Randall he had established himself in an office at No. 43 Market Street, Newark. As a precaution, however, he had boarded at Elizabeth—a few miles distant—and now advised Wales that he should come on to Jersey City by a certain date with more draft-letters. The thief was to telegraph forward when he was actually *en route*, and Dudley would be found waiting for him at Taylors' Hotel.

"As a Newark business man," wrote the scoundrel, "I have been a decided success; making friends in all quarters, and some slight acquaintance with the agents of the Express Companies. I can push the stuff through here without ruffling a feather."

The mail thief was prompt to do his part in the nefarious work. He made a fresh trip on the postal cars, and got safely to Jersey City with a number of stolen letters. In the reading-room of Taylor's Hotel he found Dudley, who at once adjourned with him to a private room. The forger then selected such drafts as could be manipulated; indorsed them to R. D. Randall, and at once took the train for Newark, and deposited them for collection in the express offices.

The preliminaries of this fraud had been carefully carried out, and the miscreants again obtained a booty of about $800 each. With certain arrangements for the future they then parted.

In a loitering, zig-zag manner, Wales started out to return to the west. At one of his sojourning places, it is needless to say which, he now seems to have met the infatuated girl whom we saw with him later on at North Adams and Boston. As her actual identity—both as to name and residence—is carefully disguised in this volume, the hope may be here expressed that Carrie Levison did not make sacrifice of her honor, except under conditions of the most trying temptation. If plausible manners, lying promises, and false pretenses as to his means and family, were the snares required to entrap this victim, the heartless libertine I am describing was fully capable of them all. Anyhow they passed a night together in a city at some distance from her father's home; and thenceforth, their illicit correspondence was continued without apparent scruple.

Passing over some of the intermediate felonies we now come to Dudley in Philadelphia, where first we met with him as T. H. Cone. From this point he forwarded to his satellite at Redrock the usual letter of advice, the same of which the envelope left its traces on the tell-tale blotting-paper.

It was now the boast of the forger that in the Quaker City he could " run things " to as large an amount as he wished, the larger the easier, and he urged upon Wales to bring on as many drafts as he could lay hands on. As we already know, he was calculating to procure an identification through the good-hearted and credulous printer in whose office he had rented his " desk-room."

Dudley's methods were again quite successful. A large sum of money was realized, and the swindlers decamped as usual; but all unconscious, of course, that these latest crimes would unleash in their pursuit the hounds of justice. On the division of the plunder Wales went to Albany, New York, where he was almost immediately joined by Dudley and his wife, the forger taking up quarters in a boarding-house under the name of W. W. Gray, and at once hiring an office in Troy as a dealer in railroad iron.

On invitation from her profligate lover, Carrie Levison also met the party at Albany; and after an interval of dissipation, in which all had some part, was taken by Wales to the dainty little village of Catskill, nestling under the mountains of the same name. After a sojourn of several days the thief left her here alone, and again returned to Redrock; having agreed to secure more drafts and rejoin Dudley in Albany.

He was entirely faithful to the villainous engagement. Taking the train, soon after, from Yarmouth, he succeeded in abstracting a number of letters; of which those containing drafts were delivered by him to Dudley at the Delavan House in Albany. It was during this trip of Wales that the reader was called on to pay his first visit to Redrock, in company with our detective, Mr. Thomas.

Next morning Dudley went over to Troy, and, as W. W. Gray, deposited drafts for $1,300 in the office of the National Express Company. A further draft for nearly $16,000 was also a part of the plunder, but of this he decided that the collection must be attempted in New York. The accomplished fraud was very well aware that its presentation at any other than a large business centre would inevitably suggest the inquiry how it came there. The transactions involving such large payments are few and far between in a place like Albany.

Meanwhile Miss Levison had remained at Catskill, and Wales proceeded by the way of that village to take her along with him to New York, where he had arranged to meet Dudley and wife at the Metropolitan Hotel on Broadway.

To insure the collection of the large draft in New York, the forger was now depending on some mercantile acquaintance in that city. At the express office, however, he was informed that the identification by this person would not be sufficient; and so leaving behind them their female companions, the disappointed swindlers hurried back again to Troy. In the latter city, by this time, the proceeds of the other drafts had been received at the express office. Procuring an identification from a hotel-keeper, at whose establishment he had frequently stopped, the daring forger received the $1,300 ; and then, without delay, put in for collection the large draft.

It was a perilous venture this, but the swindlers were now reckless, and dazed by the prospect of securing so large a booty. To anticipate, as far as possible, the risks involved, they dashed off to New York again by the night express, so that Dudley might watch at the bank next day, to see if the draft were paid. If he should notice any unusual stir on the presentation of the draft it would plainly be to their welfare that they gave Troy the cold shoulder.

In the hall of the paying bank Dudley was accordingly on hand at an early hour. On the pretense that he was waiting for a friend, he remained there much of the day ; and most of the time, even was occupied in pleasant confab with the bank detective. It was with the grace of a Chesterfield that he parted from that functionary in the afternoon ; assuring him that he would fine his friend a box of Havanas as a penalty for his lack of good faith.

At the Metropolitan he found Wales enjoying himself over some wine with two ladies.

"Well; how is it, Dud. ?" inquired the anxious letter-thief, as soon as they were alone.

"Blawst the thing," exclaimed Dudley testily, "I cawnt tell whether's it's paid or not. Several times the teller's window was so blocked up I couldn't see what checks or drafts were passed in. I certainly saw no messenger with the badge of the National Express Company."

"Let us give up the job, Dud." suggested the timorous Wales, "it's getting to be gosh-darned risky."

"No, by Jupiter!" shouted the impetuous forger; "it's not every day a fellah can make such a stake as $8,000; and I shawnt give it up without a good fight."

"Well, what can we do?" demanded the disconcerted Wales.

"I don't know what you mean to do," answered Dudley; "but for my part I'll go back to Troy and face the music."

Very willingly, indeed, would Wales have permitted his associate to challenge the danger alone, but his native cupidity soon got the better of his cowardice. He was rogue enough now to know the utter fallacy of the maxim that there is "honor among thieves." What if Dudley should abscond with the whole $16,000, to be followed by his wife to some preconcerted retreat? The bare idea of the thing was enough to set Wales almost crazy; and so he lost no time about giving his adhesion to the proposed journey. "Anyhow," thought the sneak to himself, "it is Dud. who must go to the office for the money—I shall keep under cover as much as possible."

Notwithstanding this resolve it was with a somewhat heightened pulse-beat that Wales took his seat by Dudley in the late afternoon train on the New York Central Railway. About midnight they arrived at Troy, and at once proceeded to a hotel.

The following morning, to the great horror of Wales, Dudley insisted that the latter must go down to the express office, and on some pretext of business endeavor to divine if there was anything unusual in the wind. With some trepidation the thief undertook the errand, and seeing no one around but the trustful-looking agent, inquired about a pair of boots that were to have been forwarded from New York for himself—to wit, Mr. Jeremiah Bardon. No package of the sort being discovered, Mr. Bardon launched an indignant expletive at the head of the supposed bootmaker, and then went his way to report to Dudley. The latter, meanwhile, had cautiously ascertained that no one, during his absence, had been inquiring for him, either at the hotel, or at his own little office.

On learning that the coast was entirely clear at the express office, Dudley himself now went there, and boldly inquired if the proceeds of his draft had come on.

" Yes, sir," answered the civil express agent, " the amount is here, but you understand that I cannot deliver it except on identification."

" Why," observed Dudley, " I was identified here on a draft the morning before yesterday."

" I have not forgotten you at all, Mr. Gray," said the agent, " and I am really sorry to delay your money, but my instructions from the central office refer explicitly to this draft, no doubt because the amount is unusually large."

" Oh, that's all right, my dear fellah," said Dudley, with lofty gayety; " if you are acting under instructions I would not, for the world, have you deviate from them. I shall drop in here in an hour or so with some friend who will satisfy you; there are several in the neighborhood who will gladly oblige me."

The supposed Mr. Gray then quitted the premises.

It must here be explained that the office in which the forger had been pretending to do a large business in railroad iron, was situated on the second floor of a building owned by an insurance agent named Walton. This old gentleman, with his son, had their office on the first floor, and if not very active as insurance agents, they were certainly responsible citizens—the estimate in Troy business circles being that their word was as good as their bond.

In his own high-toned, insinuating way, Dudley had become quite friendly with these gentlemen, and several times had discussed with them his intention to take out a ten-thousand-dollar life policy. As the commissions derivable from such a transaction would make quite a respectable addition to the agent's income, Mr. Walton was courtesy itself whenever Mr. Gray called in to his office. The preference given to an agent in procuring through him a policy of such magnitude, Dudley knew well to be a kind of obligation conferred. That he might at some time require a favor from this person was the motive which inspired every step of his late intercourse with him. The forger's custom, indeed, was to make friends in all directions, though the warmth of his regard for them depended entirely on whether he could use them.

And the time had now come to make use of the insurance agent.

After leaving the express office, as related, Dudley called in on the friendly Mr. Walton, whom he greeted this time with effusive warmth.

"I find I have a spare hour this morning, Mr. Walton," he said to the agent, "so I guess you can as well draw up for me the application for that policy."

"Ah! certainly; thank you, Mr. Gray; take a chair, sir; I'll attend to it at once for you," saying which the gratified agent rubbed his hands pleasantly together, and brought up the necessary blank on which such applications are drafted.

Now, Dudley was what an insurance man would call

"an excellent risk," and he quite delighted the agent by the satisfactory replies which he gave to the interrogatories in such cases made and provided. According to the inventive swindler, there was neither taint nor malady in the Gray family for many generations back, while the various grandfathers and grandmothers had, without exception, reached their four-score summers, more or less. His own personal vigor and sanitary record were likewise so presented that it was apparent his examination by the medical officers of the company would be a mere form.

"Capital life!—first-class risk!"—muttered to himself the agent, as he wrote the last entry on the record.

"Well, Mr. Walton, I can as well give you now my check for the first year's premium," next advanced Dudley, "and if the company declines the application you will, of course, refund."

This feature of the transaction was also eminently satisfactory, and Mr. Walton was the recipient of Dudley's worthless check on a Troy bank.

"Oh! by the way," next exclaimed the forger, "Walton, I have the proceeds of a draft lying in the express office beyond; would you mind stepping over that way to identify me?"

What could a poor insurance agent do? How could he refuse a business civility to the customer who was after placing in his way the handsomest commission of the season?

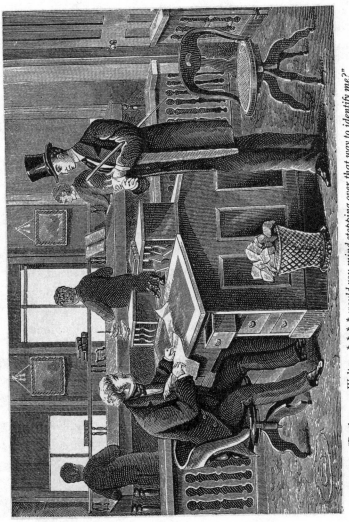

*"By the way, Walton, * * * * would you mind stepping over that way to identify me?"*

"Certainly, certainly, my dear sir, I'll do it most cheerfully," answered Mr. Walton, who was pleased indeed to have so good a risk to report to Hartford.

The obliging agent at once accompanied the forger to the express office, where Dudley had no further difficulty about obtaining and pocketing the $16,000. He now proceeded at once to where Wales was waiting for him, and together they walked down to Greenbush—a village on the east side of the Hudson, directly opposite Albany. Thence they took the cars for New York, which city they reached in perfect security.

On arrival at the Empire City, they drove to the Metropolitan Hotel, where the booty was divided in the usual way. On the following morning took place that parting in which Dudley alleged to Wales that he was going to Monroe, Michigan, since which they had neither met nor corresponded.

The reader, of course, knows that the chronicle of this felonious pair, which I have brought down to this point, was derived from the revelations of Wales after his arrival at the Philadelphia Agency. The statements in regard to Dudley may therefore be imagined to be somewhat colored. Possibly they are; for it was now an obvious advantage to Wales to have himself appear more sinned against than sinning—he the dupe, and Dudley the decoy. Of the two the latter was undoubtedly the cleverer man, and therefore competent to be the greater villain. Even on his own showing, how-

10

ever, I have done no injustice to Wales in presenting him as he is here portrayed.

With this explanation, I shall now leave him for a while in the safe and considerate care of Mr. Linden.

———◆———

CHAPTER XXVI.

The lady-like Mrs. Pelham appears in Pittsburg, and forms a Pleasant Acquaintance with Miss Lizzie Greenleaf, in whom reposes a Secret very much Desired by Mr. Pinkerton.

ONCE more I must carry my readers westward over the noble mountains, vales and rivers of Pennsylvania, and out beyond the ridges of the northern Alleghanies. The remnants of winter's snow drapery are still clinging to the hill-sides, but the April sunshine is fast brushing them away, to give place to the new vesture Spring is preparing for them. Our visit shall be to Pittsburg, the fairest in location, but swarthiest and smuttiest of Pennsylvanian cities—as may not be reproachful, however, in one which toils so sturdily, and diets so generously in coal and iron.

In one of the principal thoroughfares of this busy city might be found in those days the establishment of Dunstable Bros., extensive dealers in what are called "ladies' furnishing goods." The store was an elegant and spacious one, occupying the ground floors of two adjoining buildings, and comprising departments for wholesale as well as retail trade. Of the latter, Messrs. Dunstable had a goodly share, being usually well stocked with all the adjuncts of feminine attire, and employing quite a number of intelligent lady clerks, to exhibit and vend them to the fair dames of Pittsburg.

The great majority of their customers belonged, of course, to the gentler sex ; and these shrewd merchants understood well, that American ladies of refinement will continue to do their shopping only where they meet with a refined and sympathetic attention. In this particular trade, indeed, the duration of custom depends very much on the preference which ladies will extend to a particular assistant, whose manners and conversation may have been personally agreeable to them. Hence, almost every competent clerk has her own set of customers, and deems it her exclusive privilege to wait on any of them who may call for shopping purposes.

One afternoon in the early days of April, a lady stepped into the store of Messrs. Dunstable, who was before entirely unknown to any of their assistants. She had a youthful and pleasing face, of singularly clear and fair complexion, and enhanced in its attractiveness by full, earnest, bluish-gray eyes. Her dress was rich, without being at all pretentious ; its various constituents being presumptive rather of a quiet and perfect taste, than of a slavish devotion to prevailing fashions.

Comporting well with these surroundings was her personal demeanor, which was at once both dignified and self-contained.

The fact that this lady was not a regular customer of the establishment was testified by the inquiring manner in which she glanced along the counters at either side, as if seeking the department which might contain a certain class of goods. Noticing this hesitation, a polite lady assistant came forward to inquire her pleasure, but she merely said:

"Many thanks; I believe I now see what I want."

She then walked forward to where a young clerk was waiting alone at one of the counters. The latter was a slender and graceful girl of about nineteen summers, of not very imposing stature, but having shapely, aquiline features, and large, expressive, black eyes. She was also gifted with those rarer charms of her sex, a luxurious growth of dark glossy hair, and a white hand of perfect proportions.

Surveying her with unobtrusive interest, the visitor requested this girl to show her some varieties of hose, the counter being devoted to fabrics of that class. On this being done, she spent a few moments in selecting what she wanted, which the assistant then proceeded to make up into a parcel. When the purchase was paid for, the customer seemed on the point of addressing some sort of inquiry to the young girl, but just at the moment two very demonstrative shoppers came over to the same counter, and she confined herself to a polite remark about the weather. With a pleasant "good afternoon" she then left the store.

The following day the same lady came into Dunstable's store, and passed without any indecision along to where stood the young girl who had previously waited on her. The latter recognized her customer, and gave her a modest greeting, which was courteously acknowledged. This time the lady wanted to buy a few collars, and as there are numerous varieties of this needful little article, some time was expended in discussing styles and textures. In the course of this important negotiation, she had several times looked intently, but not rudely, into the shop girl's face, and at last put the question, apparently with deep interest:

"May I ask have you any relatives in Chicago?"

"No, madame; not any that I know of," was the placid reply.

"Dear me!" exclaimed the customer, "is it really possible? I can scarcely believe that you are not related to one of my young friends in that city. I never in all my life saw so striking a resemblance!"

The young girl smiled and blushed, as her face became the object of a fresh scrutiny, and then she ventured the inquiry:

"What is the young lady's name, please?"

"She is a Miss Nellie Forsyth," replied the customer; "and even as you ask the question, her **very** voice seems to vibrate in my ears, it is so lik**e**."

"I never even heard the name. I wish I did have a relative with such a pretty name!" naively observed the shop girl.

"Can—it—be—possible?" murmured the lady, in a meditative way; "well, well; how strangely these personal resemblances do run!"

The purchase of the collars had now been completed, and the lady seemed on the point of starting, when both together observed that it was raining. Now, for a lady out shopping to be surprised in a rain-storm, is anywhere a most vexatious circumstance; but in the good city of Pittsburg, Pennsylvania, it is nothing short of a downright calamity. The pall of bituminous smoke that hangs over its thousand furnaces is converted by the moisture into a celestial carbon factory; and from every ragged aperture thereof the soot falls down in palpable flakes, like the snow from a brooding storm-cloud. And woe betide the "love of a French hat," or the "latest thing in walking suits," that is caught abroad in the villainous downpour. Not all the skill of the modiste, nor all the secrets of chemistry would avail to restore it to its primitive luster!

It was therefore with unaffected feminine alarm that Dunstable's young assistant exclaimed to her customer:

"Oh! see how it rains, madame! your pretty cloak will be spoiled."

But the lady thus addressed had no idea whatever of permitting her dainty embroidered mantle to be ruined by the inky shower. Taking in the situation at once, she simply demanded if umbrellas were among the articles sold by Messrs. Dunstable?

Several of these useful but inconstant servitors were immediately placed on the counter, and after due inspection the lady approved and purchased a cheap one, observing, in regard to her choice, that she had an excellent umbrella at her hotel, and this one must suffice for the emergency of the moment. Once more she now turned her attention to "the article of stockings," and remarked, while selecting a further supply, that Pittsburg was "a nasty place, where one required more clean changes than anywhere she had ever been."

"Yes, *indeed*, it is," responded the shop girl; and then she added, with charming candor: "I knew you were a stranger here, madame, you are so very white!"

The lady smiled an affirmation, and again referred to the wonderful likeness of the speaker to her young Chicago friend, Nellie Forsyth.

"It seems to me as if I had known you ever so long," she said, warmly; "I cannot even yet realize that you are a stranger."

"Do you mean to stay long in Pittsburg?" timidly ventured the assistant.

"That depends on circumstances. I have been told that your smoky old city is an excellent place for business, and if I can find a good location for mine, I may stay here altogether."

"For some kinds of business it is certainly good," remarked the girl; "but others again don't seem to thrive particularly much."

"Well," said the stranger, pleasantly, "my idea was to open in the fancy goods and furnishing line, but, of course, not on such a scale as this concern—rather in a small, nice store, or even in parlors. Which do you consider the best neighborhood for such a business?"

"I should judge that you might do very well," answered the girl, "either on Market street or Fifth avenue; but you would find it difficult to get good clerks; and one, at least, you would require, who was well acquainted with the locality, to regulate your stock and purchases."

"And, by the way," she added, after a pause, "you should know that ours is also a wholesale house, and can make you as good terms as any in the trade."

"Thank you, I shall not forget that; and meanwhile I shall certainly buy of you all that I may need for my own use."

At this the zealous young clerk looked pleased, and said: "I am sure it will give me much pleasure to wait on you when you are buying; and—and I hope if you do not see me in the store you will ask for me."

Hereupon she took out a neat little card-case, and handed the customer her card. The latter accepted it

She took out a neat little card-case and handed the customer her card.

very graciously, and quickly glanced down to read the name which was engraved on it—

Miss Lizzie Greenleaf.

The conversation was then prolonged for a few minutes, during which the lady stated that her own name was Mrs. Cornelia Pelham, and that she was temporarily staying at the Diamond Hotel.

"I believe I must make a change soon," she added, "for it is quite an expensive house, and I may be a long time before I find the right location for my business. Do you know of any good hotel that is really comfortable, and likely to be more moderate? I should rely very much on your judgment in the matter."

Miss Greenleaf shook her head.

"I know scarcely anything about the prices," she said; "but I think you would find the Central a comfortable house; or the Alleghany City, if you didn't mind crossing the river a little."

"No; but there is no hurry whatever," said the lady; "I shall probably inquire about those you have mentioned; and I *do* hope, Miss Greenleaf, that when I am settled down you will come to see me?"

This kindly invitation was acknowledged in a suitable manner, and the rain having considerably abated, the lady soon took her departure.

In her apartment at the Diamond Hotel, Mrs. Pelham was shortly very busy writing for my Agency

10*

an accurate report of her interview with Lizzie Greenleaf, and the prospects of its leading to a serviceable
intimacy.

Immediately on learning of Wales's confession, I
had urged on Mr. Bangs the necessity of "shadowing"
Dudley's sister-in-law, whose correspondence with his
wife seemed the only chain that bound that couple
with the outer world. Wherever their retreat might
be, Miss Greenleaf would surely know it; and until
we had in some way wormed out this secret, she must
become for us an object of special solicitude. But as
it was quite unlikely that the young lady's correspondence would be made known to an ordinary detective,
it was decided to bring in contact with her a person of
her own sex; one who might from ordinary business
acquaintance push on into the intimacy of friendship,
and ultimately into such close confidence as might enable her to obtain the coveted address.

For this delicate mission I had designed Mrs.
Pelham, a New York lady of high culture and respectability, who had before rendered signal services to
justice in operations on which I had employed her.
With Officer Delaney as an escort, the lady was at once
dispatched to Pittsburg, where both took up quarters
at the Diamond Hotel; but independently, and as if
entire strangers to each other. Provided by Wales
with the address and description of Miss Greenleaf,
Mr. Bangs had instructed Delaney to first discover and

identify that young lady, and next to point her out to Mrs. Pelham. The latter was then to employ the best available means of making her acquaintance ; only anything like a formal introduction was to be avoided, as likely to arouse suspicion on the part of a young person who was presumed to be on her guard, and perhaps keenly alive to the fact that her sister's husband was hiding from justice.

In the first two days after their arrival at the Diamond, Delaney had acceptably performed his part of singling out Miss Greenleaf among the numerous clerks at Dunstable's. In point of fact he had recognized her at once from the description given by Wales ; and had graven every feature in his memory during a very deliberate investment in a new pocket-handkerchief. That he was quite correct was only proven, when, in the evening, he shadowed the same young lady home, and learned that the house which she entered was that of Mr. H. S. Dryer—a name which Wales had given us as that of Miss Greenleaf's maternal uncle.

Delaney was waiting for the opportunity to point her out to Mrs. Pelham, when that competent lady took the task in her own hands, and in the manner we have seen, not only discovered who Miss Greenleaf was, but dug deeply into the trench that was to undermine her secret.

CHAPTER XXVII.

A Long and Discouraging Search for the Forger, Dudley.

WHILE thus groping for light in the murky atmosphere of Pittsburg, the Agency had by no means been idle in other directions. The very evening when he had received Wales's confession, Mr. Bangs dispatched Officer Thomas to Monroe, Michigan, where Dudley told Wales he was going to settle down. The description of his forger-confederate, which had been obtained from the latter, was minute even to redundance ; and was further remarkable from the fact, observed by the General Superintendent, that, while none of the descriptions from outside parties exactly agreed with it, it embodied nearly all the specialties mentioned in each of them. The description of Mrs. Dudley was also very precise ; the personal appearance, dress, and adornments of the lady being catalogued most faithfully, down, even, to her bonnet trimmings and finger-rings. But the most signal means to their identification seemed to consist in the baggage that accompanied them, which Wales affirmed to consist invariably of two large trunks—one Saratoga make, and one gentleman's—a black leather valise, and a plain, white-wood hat-box, about twelve inches square. They also had with them, Wales said, a handsome, brass-wire

bird-cage, containing a canary; the cage being sometimes carried in a brown linen bag, and usually deco-
rated the window of the apartment in which the pair
sojourned.

With this remarkable hat-box and bird-cage ever in
his mind's eye, Mr. Thomas had started out in his new
pursuit of the forger. It was part of the detective's
instructions to take in on this journey the cities of
Cleveland and Yarmouth, so as to make inquiries at the
post-offices for letters for Wales. It had been the practice of Dudley, the captive told us, to address him at
either of those cities when there was swindling work to
be done; the risk of sending letters for him direct to
his own home being sufficiently obvious.

Thomas found there were no letters at either of those
places, and so telegraphed to the Agency; with the additional news from Yarmouth that a rumor of Wales's
arrest had somehow got afloat in that city. Nobody
with whom he had spoken, however, could tell where
it originated, and none seemed to know by whom, or
where, the thief was held captive. But the fact that it
had leaked out at all, and might therefore reach the
ears of Dudley, was sufficiently alarming to intensify
the anxiety of Thomas. That diligent officer was now
more than ever warmed in his eager pursuit; or as he
himself quaintly reported, "I never so desired to meet
with a living person, as I do at present with R. L.
Dudley."

At Monroe the detective's first step was to make a quiet search in the two or three modest hotels which the place contained. Not the smallest clue to the whereabouts of Dudley and wife was found at either of them; and no one about the depot, livery stables, express offices, or other resorts of travelers, had noticed the arrival of any such party. For a town of *its* limited extent, where every intelligent citizen seemed to know everybody else, this might have been considered sufficient. But Thomas also spent a couple of toilsome days inquiring along the streets, and almost from house to house, for the married couple recently arrived, whose baggage included a white-wood hat-box, and a brass canary cage. Nor did he even neglect the older quarter of the town, where the high-peaked gables and iron shutters of the dwellings gave token of their French construction. Nobody had seen the Dudleys though—nobody had heard of them—and not even a single canary cage, hanging by a window, relieved the barren monotony of the search.

Becoming quite concerned at the intelligence that no trace had been found at Monroe, and at the impending risk that Dudley might learn of the capture of his accomplice, I now hastened to the East to confer with my General Superintendent on the adoption of a more energetic course. The immediate consequence was, that Mr. Bangs took specially into his own hands the task of instructing our ambassadress at Pittsburg;

while Linden was enjoined to hold Thomas in constant intercourse, and direct his movements in the personal search for the forgers.

At Monroe, accordingly, that disappointed officer received the order from his superintendent to lose not a moment's time, but continue the pursuit in Detroit and Kalamazoo, both in the same State. To the former beautiful city Thomas at once repaired, and for three whole days made diligent search and inquiry at its various hotels, depots, ferries, and express offices. But there was no sign whatever of Dudley and his wife; and not a glimpse was vouchsafed to the detective, nor a tradition reached him, of their yellow metallic cage. No better fortune attended him at Kalamazoo, from which point he telegraphed to Mr. Linden, that unless a fresh trail were struck, the search must be carried on under terrible disadvantages. By this time he had come to learn that very few persons indeed were likely to recall the belongings of a passing traveler, whom they had encountered only once, about six weeks before.

But it was not the privilege of Mr. Thomas to re-pine at the difficulties of the task to which he was assigned. On other shoulders than his lay the burden of the operation, and in other intellects the genius to make it successful. Old trail, or fresh trail, or no trail at all, his simple duty was to carry out orders. Nothing, therefore, was left him, but implicit obedience, when he received from Mr. Linden instructions to return at once to Detroit, and take up the chase after the forger along the Grand Trunk Railway of Canada, visiting on his route such places as Port Huron, Sarnia, Stratford, Brampton, Guelph, Toronto, Port Hope, Colburg, Kingston, Ottawa, Prescott and Montreal. His inquiries after Dudley and wife were to be of the most thorough kind, and to extend themselves down to conductors, hotel-porters, and news agents, at all the points named. To these various classes of persons he was to describe the peculiar baggage of the fugitives, on the chance that it might be remembered where all ordinary signals were forgotten. The detective was to push on quickly; make a daily report by telegraph; and look out for dispatches at every point named, besides calling for letters at the post-office in Toronto.

In compliance with his instructions, Mr. Thomas took the first train for Detroit, but found no opportunity of proceeding further until seven o'clock of the following morning. He then took the cars for Port Huron, and after a diligent inquisition in that place, crossed the river St. Clair to Sarnia, where for the first time our operation had extended outside the boundaries of the country.

Nothing whatever came of the detective's efforts at the two places named, and it was half-past ten o'clock at night when he arrived quite weary at the depot of Stratford, a pretty Canadian town, which is named after Shakspeare's birth-place, and like it, is situated on a gentle river Avon.

In the morning early Thomas was afoot, but his researches in Stratford having no better result than elsewhere, he left at nine o'clock, and stopping at Guelph on the way, succeeded by the early afternoon in reaching Brampton, a cozy little village about thirty miles west of Toronto.

In his usual call at the telegraph office here, Mr. Thomas received no dispatches, but later in the day he had the happy thought to send back to Stratford the inquiry whether any had arrived since morning. Such proved to be the case, and he had the telegram repeated on to Brampton, where it was delivered to him as follows :

" Go to Albany, New York, at once, and telegraph on your arrival.　　　　R. J. LINDEN."

As soon as he could get another train, the detective started for Toronto, which he only reached at eleven o'clock at night, and was compelled to remain over till morning. Crossing next day from Toronto into the United States, Thomas took train at Suspension Bridge, and was soon dashing along on the New York Central towards the legislative capital of the Empire State. He was not destined, however, to any long detention at Albany, for about noon he heard a conductor pass through the cars inquiring if Mr. J. R. Thomas was aboard.

"That's my name," said the detective, looking up from his newspaper.

Hereupon the conductor handed him a telegram on which was written :

"Find J. R. Thomas on train, and instruct him to go through to Boston to-night."

This the detective did, and arrived in Boston about two o'clock in the afternoon of the following day. At the office of the Adams' Express Company he found a letter from Mr. Linden, with full explanation of the move, and a programme of fresh work.

It had been ascertained from Pittsburg, wrote Mr. Linden, that Dudley was assuredly in Boston, and had been there since April 1st—it was now the 18th—being on that date in some one of the hotels. Thomas was now required to visit every hotel in the modern Athens, examine all the registers for Dudley's hand-writing, and, by inquiries from porters and others, endeavor to trace the forger and his wife by their peculiar baggage.

That my readers may be enlightened as to how the Agency became possessed of this information, they must turn with me once more to Pittsburg, and to the detectives, male and female, who were working for us at that point.

CHAPTER XXVIII.

An extraordinary Surveillance, and the Reasons therefor.— Touching Forbidden Ground.—An agreeable Interchange of Gossip resulting in Mrs. Pelham securing some valuable Information.

A S might readily be supposed, the course of Mrs. Pelham's intimacy with Lizzie Greenleaf was quite at the mercy of circumstances, and mainly, indeed, of that very changeful commodity, known as "woman's fancy." The line of Mr. Delaney's duty, however, was much more definite. Early every morning from the time at which he had identified her, he waited on the street near Mr. Dryer's house to watch the young store clerk come forth to her daily task. As she always took the street-cars to go down town it became the practice of the detective to ride on the conveyance with her, and sometimes on the same seat, until she was duly deposited near Dunstable's establishment.

To avoid the danger of being specially remarked by her, Delaney sometimes rode on the front platform, and sometimes on the rear ; sometimes got on at one point, and sometimes at another ; concealing his identity by the use of simple, but effectual disguises. When the lady had got to work, he would remain within sight of the store until the dinner-hour. If she came out at noon he would follow her; note where she stopped or loitered; whom she saluted or spoke with; what papers or parcels she carried; and every other detail, however minute, that contributed to the total of her visible out-door life. At evening, in like manner, he would review from safe ambush the exodus of the young ladies who worked for Messrs. Dunstable; and having seen Miss Greenleaf into the crowded street-car, would screen himself in some obscure corner thereof, until after she had descended at Mr. Dryer's door. Nor would he forsake that interesting locality until the lateness of the hour, and the extinguishment of the hall lamp, gave ground for the assurance that the household had all retired. From some of that officer's reports, indeed,—which are before me as I write,—I am reminded that this pertinacious shadow duty was several times performed during hours of pelting rain, and of nights, when the stormy obscurity made it necessary to stand close by Mr. Dryer's railing, to examine such persons as might enter or leave the premises.

But my readers would fail to understand the value of this extraordinary surveillance, unless they were told a few of its advantages. Let me summarize them briefly.

In less than ten days from her arrival in Pittsburg Mrs. Pelham had been informed, outside her own observation, that Miss Lizzie Greenleaf was really a modest and circumspect little lady; that she saw scarcely any society, made no visits herself, and had no other

visitors than those of her uncle; that tne friends of the
latter were among the most refined people in Pittsburg; and that theie were no boarders in his house,
and no chance for a lady to obtain board thereat. She
had also learned that Lizzie attended a Methodist
church near her residence; that she had personally
mailed no letters within those ten days; and that she
was very fond of reading, and favored certain books
and periodicals—this last being a street-car observation.

Of her personal habits it had likewise been noted
that she generally brought a little lunch to the store
with her; that she was partial to toast and cold broiled
chicken; that when she omitted to bring lunch she took
a walk out at noon to Alleghany City, and dined at
Dr. Marsh's, in Lacock Street; that the doctor's wife
was her sister; and that she sometimes dropped in there
at noon or eventide, when a visit seemed uncalled for
as a dietetic necessity.

Trivial and unobjective as many of these things
would seem, they were not without importance to the
lady at the Diamond Hotel, who heard them from
Delaney by daily installments. They were likewise of
much significance to Messrs. Bangs and Linden, whom
they satisfied that Dudley and his wife were certainly
not at Pittsburg; that they could not come there without our knowing it; and that whatever their correspondence with Lizzie Greenleaf, she was not a young

person to go shouting it out in the public market-place.

But Delaney was now instructed to go a step further. The faithful little clerk was so punctual and attentive to her business, that he might safely spend elsewhere the hours between her morning arrival and the time for her noonday meal. Among many other duties Mr. Bangs prescribed for him during these intervals was to examine the delivery books at the express offices. Scarcely had he begun this task when he discovered that on the third of April Miss Greenleaf had received through the Adams' Express a Boston parcel, on which she had to pay the transportation charge. The date and way-bill number of this parcel were at once telegraphed to the Agency, and Mr. Bangs telegraphed to Boston to see if the Express Company could learn the name of the sender. The reply was unsatisfactory; the only thing that was learned being, that the parcel was handed in at the Boston office by some unknown and forgotten person.

Meanwhile the diplomacy of Mrs. Pelham was tending to more positive results. After the interview with Miss Greanleaf in which she obtained her card, she did not consider it politic to call very soon. A couple of days were now usefully spent in examining vacant stores, so as to be furnished with material for future conferences. The project of starting a place of business was not altogether a fictitious one; even its continuance for some months was within the range of our calculations. It was simply one of several such plans which Mr. Bangs had outlined, to be chosen from and acted on, as events might render necessary. Should our researches in all other directions continue to prove abortive, the sister-in-law of the forger would at last become our sheet anchor. No ordinary outlay of time and ingenuity should be spared to make her a safe and strong one.

The second afternoon from the interview already detailed, Mrs. Pelham called in at Dunstable's to "prospect" in some black silks. When she entered the store Miss Greenleaf was quite busy, but she soon made an opportunity to come over to her new customer; apologizing, as she came, for having kept her so long waiting. Mrs. Pelham responded with a pleasantry, and a very agreeable conversation was started over the silks, when a large influx of customers apprised her that it was untimely. On one pretext or another she decided that she would not make her selection just then: but managed to convey to Miss Greenleaf that she would very probably be changing to the Central Hotel, and hoped she would drop in there some time and have a little dinner with her. The girl seemed flattered by the invitation, her own last words being a gage of reciprocity :

"Come into the store any time you are passing," she said ; "I'm sure I shall be very glad to see you !"

But two more days were permitted to elapse before Mrs. Pelham again called. It was now Saturday afternoon, and in those very quiet hours which from time immemorial the ladies have consecrated to shopping: that is, not at the mere behest of so many vulgar necessities, but for the agonizing pleasure of being tempted by costly luxuries.

Miss Greenleaf seemed much pleased at her visit, and exclaimed quite gayly:

"I was just thinking of you, Mrs. Pelham, and as you didn't call these two days, I was wondering if you hadn't got tired of smoky Pittsburg."

"Oh! no—not quite—but it really *is* a dirty place; I declare to you I am kept quite busy washing my hands, and changing collars and cuffs, and yet I never seem to feel quite right!"

Miss Greenleaf laughed.

'I have a sister," she observed, "who complains of it just like you; and I was often indignant at it until I went to New York to see her; but indeed I found everything there *so* clean that I didn't wonder any more."

"You have traveled a little, then?" suggested Mrs. Pelham, inquiringly.

"Very little, indeed," was the somewhat regretful answer; "it was quite an uncommon treat to me to get that week last winter which I spent with sister at her boarding-house in New York. That city is so—— oh! by the way, did you see the nice little store which is just finishing on Penn street?"

The interruption to these personalities, so quickly

sprung, immediately struck Mrs. Pelham as a clever after-thought, as if Lizzie had remembered herself as touching on forbidden ground. The lady made no sign of having noticed it.

" Yes, I was in it," she quietly answered, "but the gentleman informs me that it is already rented. However, I don't think I need hurry myself,—I seem to be rather late for the spring trade, and my time will not be entirely lost, since I am making many useful acquaintances."

" Have you changed your boarding-place yet?"

" Not yet; I find the Central is awfully dear,—four and a half to five dollars a day. I am beginning to think that a nice boarding-house will suit me best."

This was dropped out in the hope that Lizzie might name one, or at least interest herself in the selection. But she made no comment whatever, and Mrs. Pelham now fell back on the actual business of purchasing her dress goods, and only ventured to say, before leaving:

" Do come and have dinner with me to-morrow, Miss Greenleaf; I shall begin to feel like a hermit for want of some friendly face to look at across the table."

" Oh! I am really sorry," answered the good-natured girl; " I had already engaged to dine at my sister's in Alleghany City; she is quite sick at present, and her husband, Dr. Marsh, insisted on my coming."

" Well, well," said Mrs. Pelham, resignedly, " I am

11

doomed to a lonely Sunday, I see; but I shall reckon on your company at another time, mind."

With a pleasant "good-bye," she then left the store.

Sunday was really a dull day for Mrs. Pelham, and in the afternoon she took refuge in her room and in the companionship of an interesting book. About three o'clock she was disturbed by a knock at the door, on opening which she found Miss Greenleaf, radiant as a little spring blossom, and laughing with girlish glee at the notion of having surprised her.

"So I have come to see you after all," she exclaimed, as Mrs. Pelham seized her hands and saluted her warmly.

"Oh! you are most welcome," said the latter; "it is *so* kind of you to come to visit a poor lonely woman, and I have been feeling very badly all day, too. Sit down, sit down, my dear, and let me take off your things."

While insisting that she could not remain long, the girl surrendered her hat and sacque, and her hostess proceeded to make her "at home" by all the little arts pertaining to female hospitality. The visitor had dined, of course, being just on her return from Alleghany City; but she could not refuse the ever-timely tea, which is as much a woman's festal draught as it is her daily solace. A cozy little tea was soon served in the room, and the generous aroma floated softly upward

from a table which was garnished with cakes, fruit-pre-
serves, and other such "fixins"—besides a solid reserve
of *toast and cold broiled chicken!*

Conversation over this impromptu banquet soon became animated, and, as is generally the case between
friends of the sex, it dallied and coquetted with topics
as various as bees might sip flowers in an Illinois
prairie. The portions of it that concerned our operation may be extracted without scruple; for so little of
continuity was there in any direction, that its beginning might be found anywhere, and its ending not
at all.

"How do you like Pittsburg by this time?" inquired
Miss Greenleaf, at one point; "for *my* part I am tired to
death of it,—it is *so* slow to be always living in one
place."

"I begin to like it very well now," said Mrs Pelham, "but of course I am still feeling lonesome, and
shall do so, I presume, until I have my hands full of
business."

"Wouldn't it be nice if you had some relative with
you?—is your mother alive?"

"No; she has been dead many years. The only
near lady relative I have is one married sister. You
have sisters too, have you not?"

"Yes, three of them," answered Lizzie; "we are
four in all; Mrs. Marsh, the doctor's wife, who is the
eldest; Mrs. Savis, who lives here in Pittsburg; and

sister Etta, who is next to me, and almost my very picture."

"Three of you are neighbors then, and one an absentee?" observed the hostess with placid interest.

"Yes; Etta is traveling most of the time."

"Her husband is a traveler, I suppose?"

"He is, and she goes *every*-where with him."

"How very, *very* pleasant that must be for her; there are so many brutes of traveling men who never once think to take their wives along!"

"Oh! sister wouldn't stay at home, bless you—she wouldn't let him go without her!"

"Indeed!" said Mrs. Pelham, laughing; "well, if she be as good as you are, I know she cannot be jealous of him;—but he must have a very good salary to take her with him all the time?—or, does he travel for himself?"

Lizzie seemed to hesitate for an answer, but it came forth quite tranquilly as she laid down her teacup:

"Not for himself—he is 'drumming' for some house in New York."

"And does your sister never pass a season in Pittsburg with you?"

"No; she got married some time after mamma's death,—which happened nearly four years ago,—and she has never once been back since."

"Dearie me! you will soon forget each other," suggested Mrs. Pelham.

"Indeed, I hope not, Mrs. Pelham! we are too much attached for that. Only think,—I love her better than *all* the rest! I made her a visit in New York last winter, but could only stay a few days. We had a very pleasant time of it, though; brother-in-law took us to *so* many places;—he is a perfectly splendid fellow for showing one around!"

"Well, I suppose it is the same as your own family, to be living with your aunt?"

"Oh! Mrs. Dryer is not an aunt, although we always call her so; she was only poor mamma's first cousin."

"I shall not be much longer with her," added the young girl, after a pause; "for grandmamma has built a nice little house on the Cumberland Valley line, and I am going to stay with her, and come in to my business every morning on the train."

"Ah! you will surely feel dull in a country house —won't you?"

"No, no; sister Marcella—that's Mrs. Savis—is coming out to stay with us for the summer, and she has two little children, such pretty darlings they are!"

A digression here followed on the old theme of family resemblances, in the course of which Mrs. Pelham learned that Mrs. Savis was fair and blue-eyed, and the other three sisters—including her informant —were dark, and very much alike; the resemblance between herself and Etta being eminently striking.

"Where is Etta now?" said Mrs. Pelham, with an air of supreme unconcern, although a correct answer to the question would have gratified many aspirations.

"I—don't—know; I wish I could hear from her," responded Lizzie, slowly, but with apparent candor; "she keeps moving about so much that our correspondence has become quite irregular; though, indeed, I am always anxious to hear from her."

"How provoking not to hear from one's friends in a long time like that!" threw out Mrs. Pelham.

"Oh! it's not so very long,—only a few days ago, —and got a parcel from her as well. She was then in Boston; and said they were going to keep house and stay all summer—but I mean they are such vagrants I shall not know for sure till I get another letter or parcel."

It is needless to say that in the course of this desultory talk Mrs. Pelham had to encounter quite a number of questions in regard to herself or her connections, real or fictitious. With *her* statements, however, this narrative has no concern; except to mention that the agreeable interchange occupied the ladies up to five o'clock.

At that point Lizzie arose, and said she must now leave, as the cars always got crowded towards supper time on Sundays. Her grateful hostess insisted that she would herself see her home; and at once rang her bell to have a carriage provided. In this the two ladies took a short ride around before proceeding toward Mr. Dryer's. Mrs. Pelham learned nothing new, however, in the balance of their chat, and deposited Miss Greenleaf at the door of her residence, apparently charmed with her new-found friend.

The reader may have noticed that during the entire evening Miss Lizzie had never named her absent sister as Mrs. Dudley, nor, indeed, used the name at all; and that Mrs. Pelham had as wisely refrained from asking her for the marriage name of Etta. The conviction of this lady was not less strong, that Etta and the forger's wife were one, and as soon as she could reach the telegraph office, she communicated to Mr. Linden the results of her evening's progress.

* * *

CHAPTER XXIX.

" Taking Reckonings."—A Little Ruse and its Lamentable Failure.— The Intimacy between Mrs. Pelham and Lizzie Greenleaf is Increased.

LET us now, as the seamen say, "take reckonings." Dudley was in Boston.

Of the three hundred thousand persons who made that city their abiding-place, the forger was one—a mere obscure unit—and a slippery and skulking one at that.

Really that seems about all—and the total is rather a slender one to boast of.

It is true that this Dudley had his wife with him ; also a peculiar hat-box, and a singing canary in a brass cage. But as a means to his discovery what even of that ? What multitudes of honorable Bostonians were dwellers in the tents of matrimony ! How numerous must be the home circles—if even we could invade them—in which singing canaries were cherished pets ! And where in this proud Cradle of Liberty, this nursery of all the proprieties, could we hope to find citizens so obliging as to hang out their hat-boxes for our inspection ?

We leave Mr. Thomas for a while to grapple with these conundrums, and return once more to our Superintendent in Philadelphia. The first and most obvious need of Mr. Linden was to know if this intelligence were really correct ;—*had Lizzie Greenleaf spoken the truth ?* Little as it was to know, and know only, that Dudley was in Boston, it was of paramount importance to verify even that. To obtain this verification, and to ascertain, if possible, the forger's full address, was the design of a little plot which was now contrived in the Quaker City.

From the time of his detention at the Agency, Wales had been permitted a free intercourse by letter with his brother at Redrock and with Carrie Levison. His communications were always dated as from the " American Hotel, Philadelphia ;" and the answers coming for

him were procured by my officers at an establishment so
named.   The entire correspondence, of course, had to
pass through Mr. Linden's hands ; who assured himself
that his prisoner did not disclose his actual situation,
and thereby give the signal for Dudley to escape.   But
knowing very well that such a proceeding would at
once put an end to his correspondence, Wales made no
attempt to abuse his privilege.   In regard to warning
Dudley, indeed, it is likely he would be the last to think
of it ; as, for reasons already set forth, he was as anxious
as could be for his early capture, and more so from day
to day as his own confinement became more irksome.

It was now suggested to the captive that he write a
confidential letter to Lizzie, so as to obtain from her, as
his friend, Dudley's exact address.   As she well knew
of their confederacy, and as we now learned, even of
its criminal character, it seemed quite improbable that
she would refuse to Wales what she was careful to
withhold from a stranger like Mrs. Pelham.   To account for his being in Philadelphia, and for his anxiety
to obtain the address, the captive was permitted to use
his own invention.   Thereupon he wrote the following
letter, which Mr. Linden approved and dispatched to
Pittsburg :

FRIEND LIZZIE :

No doubt you will be surprised at getting a letter
from me after so long an absence , still, I have not for-

11*

gotten you as a friend, and, more than that, a secret friend. I am now about to ask you a favor that will never be forgotten either by me or Dudley. He and I did a job at Troy, New York, last February, and they have finally got me, but will let me go if I settle up with one of the parties,—but I lack five hundred dollars of it. Now, if I can get a letter to Dudley without any one knowing his whereabouts, he can and will most willingly send me the money. At present I do not know where he is, and he does not know of my whereabouts.

This present letter I had a friend mail without any one knowing it; and you can safely address me as Harry Norman, Continental Hotel, giving me Dudley's address, which is the *favor* I earnestly beg of you.

Yours, truly,
W. R. WALES (or HARRY).

The reply to this letter was eagerly awaited at Philadelphia, where everything was hoped from it. In about three days it reached the Superintendent's hands, to the following effect:

DEAR HARRY:

I received your letter, and am very sorry I cannot do the favor you ask of me, as I am as ignorant of the whereabouts of those you inquired about as yourself. I have not had a letter from them since before Christmas, and have not the slightest idea where they are.—

I am sorry to hear of your misfortune, and hope you will find some other plan of escape, as it would not be safe to depend upon hearing anything, for I may not hear from them in a long time. I at once destroyed your letter, as I did not like keeping it in my possession; some one might read it. I am sorry that my reply will not be very interesting or encouraging to you at the present time.

You have my best wishes for your future welfare, and I hope you will be safe by the time I hear from you again.

I remain your friend,

Lizzie.

So far as its immediate purpose was concerned, this correspondence was a lamentable failure; but it threw a world of valuable light on the relations which Miss Greenleaf must henceforth bear to our operations. It will be quite plain to my readers, as it then became to us, that we had no mere plastic or nerveless subject in this shop girl, still in her teens. This one brief letter to Wales, in fact, established beyond a doubt that Lizzie Greenleaf was a clever, wide-awake, and resolute woman, not without some knowledge of "ways that are dark;" and one who, though she might little sympathize with a deed of forgery, was determined not to endanger the secret of Dudley. His crimes, indeed, might be abhorrent to her nature, but the criminal was the husband of her favorite sister,—and in this appeared the motive of her shrewdness and her strength.

As a hint for her own guidance, and a spur to her ingenuity, the account of this correspondence was at once furnished to Mrs. Pelham ; to whose efforts in Pittsburg we shall now again revert.

From the Sunday of Miss Greenleaf's visit to her room at the Diamond, the calls of Mrs. Pelham at Dunstable's store continued with sufficient regularity. During one which she made in the ensuing week, the statement that Etta and her husband were living in Boston was again made by Lizzie, and this time under such circumstances as permitted no reasonable doubt of its correctness.

This particular morning Mrs. Pelham had first asked to see some cloth, of a kind which she knew was not kept at Dunstable's. She then inquired for certain trimmings, and while occupied in their examination, maintained a lively conversation about the weather, the fashions, and other staples of feminine interest. The first attempt to give it a personal bearing was an inquiry by the lady after the health of Lizzie's sister in Alleghany City, Mrs. Dr. Marsh.

"Thank you, she is feeling much better this week," replied Lizzie, "and we expect she will be able to move into the country in a few days."

After this there was an interval of awkward con straint, which Mrs. Pelham dared not break by a ven

ture of the same kind. Apprised as she had just been
of the failure of the Wales' letter, she was trebly on
the alert against arousing the suspicions of the wary
young store-clerk. To do so at this juncture would be
to imperil all she had gained, and perhaps to ruin the
entire operation.

Almost in despair, and on the point of leaving the
store, she now happily bethought her that she wanted
to buy a parasol. A fresh invoice of these articles had
just come to hand, and some minutes were now spent
in discussing the new styles. While the pair were thus
engaged, Lizzie chanced to mention that she had lost
her own parasol on the Sunday previous.

" Indeed !" exclaimed Mrs. Pelham, " where did
you lose it, dear ?"

" I am not very sure," answered the girl, " but I
think I must have dropped it either while getting into,
or out of, the carriage in which we went riding. I
certainly had it when we came down stairs from your
room."

Mrs. Pelham at once took the blame of this loss to
herself, and urged, that as she had insisted on her
taking the carriage ride, she must be permitted to replace the article lost on the occasion. Lizzie protested
somewhat, but finally accepted, and with manifest
pleasure, the handsome parasol which the lady selected
for her.

An animated gossip was thus again brought about,

and presuming the field to be clear, Mrs. Pelham hazarded a question :

" Have you heard from your other sister yet,—the one from whom you were expecting a letter ?"

She had not looked up at Lizzie while speaking, but she at once noticed the unreadiness or hesitation of the girl in furnishing the answer. Without waiting for it at all, she dashed on again, just as if it was of no earthly consequence, and as if the question was merely the prelude to her own communication.

"I had a letter from *my* sister this morning," she continued, " and she implores me not to get so deeply engaged in business that I cannot go East with her this summer. She is going on a visit to Boston, and says that I must be ready to make the trip, and that—"

This time Mrs. Pelham was looking direct into the sweet face of the girl, and could trace the opening expression of interest that brightened by degrees into pleasurable sympathy, and almost into excitement.

" Why !" burst out Lizzie at this point, " I expect to go to Boston myself ! I had a long letter yesterday from sister Etta, and she writes me that they are now settled down in Boston for the summer, and want me ever so bad to pay them a visit."

" Ah ! indeed; that's nice,—and does sister like it ?"

" She seems to like it much; she and her husband

both write very pleasantly of it. I must certainly try and go there in the dull season."

Mrs. Pelham here became bold,—perilously bold.

"What part of Boston does your sister live in?—I mean in what street—do you know?"

"No,—they didn't mention it," answered Lizzie, looking calmly at the questioner out of her grand, dark eyes.

The eyes which they encountered, however, were quite as fathomless and as tranquil-looking as the girl's.

"Because," said Mrs. Pelham, continuing as if in explanation of her question, "I have been several times in Boston myself, and have quite a number of friends there; but I like Charlestown better to live in."

The disembarrassed gossip now again wandered to indifferent topics, until, discovering it was near dinner time, Mrs. Pelham left with a pleasantly renewed invitation from Lizzie not to spare her visits.

Nor did she thenceforward; although she began to remark with great anxiety that Lizzie had never extended an invitation to her to call at her own home. As subsequently transpired, however, this was attributable to domestic causes; the young girl's relations with the Dryer family being somewhat infelicitous. Of her feelings in regard to Etta's husband, Mrs. Pelham had concluded at this time that Lizzie liked Dudley very well, and would do all she could to help or screen him, but that she realized keenly the disgrace and danger of his alliance with the family.

At this point also, Mr. Bangs instructed our clever embassadress not to risk too much on direct or personal questions, but to cultivate her ripening intimacy in patience, and maintain by every precaution, and at all hazards, the vantage ground she had so adroitly won.

CHAPTER XXX.

Detective Thomas in Boston.— Plenty of Traces, but no tangible Discoveries.

ANIMATED and inspired by his chief at Philadelphia, Mr. Thomas had entered on the campaign in Boston. It would but weary my reader were I to reproduce *in extenso* the instructions by which he was now guided. But they were more ample and comprehensive than all that had preceded them ; and they were amended and revised daily through the sleepless vigilance of Mr. Linden.

Equally wearisome, perhaps, would it be, to recount in detail the movements of the detective himself. He hardly seemed to need the stimulus which the superintendent so regularly and so conscientiously applied. His own zeal as an officer had warmed into genuine en-

thusiasm ; and even the vexation which he felt at repeated mishaps, but served to intensify the energy of
his pursuit.

It took the officer several days to examine the
registers of all the known hotels in Boston; his attention being more specially directed to the dates succeeding that on which the forger had left New York. It
is scarcely necessary to state that he found no entry of
" R. L. Dudley and wife," nor of any other man and
wife whose registration bore evidence of having been
traced by the hand of Dudley.

The verbal inquiries which he made at the same
time were for a young married couple—whom he would
describe—who had arrived about four weeks previously, accompanied by such and such peculiar baggage,—
which he would also describe. But all such perquisi-
tions were equally fruitless. Neither landlords nor
clerks, porters nor hackmen, expressmen nor omnibus
drivers, had the smallest recollection of this couple, nor
of the two trunks, nor the hat-box, nor the cage.

" The parties didn't stop here, sir ;—we couldn't
fail to have remarked such baggage," was the average
reply of one class.

" Well, misther, it's not so aisy to keep thrack for a
whole month; but if I handled such thraps as thim, I'd
remimber thim till Tibbs' Eve," was the frequent re-
joinder among the other.

Succeeding this unprofitable hotel search came a

diligent tour of inquiry at the railroad depots, in which baggage-masters, clerks, "baggage smashers," and others of that ilk were catechised by Thomas to the limits of their curt endurance. Through the incivility and rudeness of some, and the stupidity of many, this was quite frequently a mortifying experience; but the detective had steeled himself alike against ignorance and insolence. In the further distance he saw only that hat-box, and and that bird-cage,—with the forger near by,—and an avalanche of obstacles would not have swerved him from his course.

This dogged perseverance at last found some recompense. At the Old Colony depot he one day encountered a baggage-clerk who *did* remember scme baggage of that kind.

"You do, eh?" persisted Thomas, again minutely describing the articles.

"Yes, sir; that's just the lot,—two big trunks, hat-box, and bird-cage in a bag. They came from New York about four weeks ago on the morning express."

"Did you see the owners?—do you know where the things went?"

"No; I took no notice of the passengers, but I remember the baggage quite well. It lay in the shed there for three or four hours, and was then removed in some kind of conveyance, I don't know what, or where."

This was all that could be learned at this point, and

now again came the tug of war for Thomas. Who took that baggage from the Old Colony depot ?—and whither it was taken ?

In vain did the detective exert himself to procure the answers to these questions. In vain again did he circulate through Boston like a walking sign of interrogation. The officials and hangers-on at the depots were re-interviewed; the hotels were revisited; the livery-stables and express offices were ransacked—but no trace of the baggage could anywhere be found. Even the newsvenders and pea-nut merchants were appealed to for light, but none of them had observed the transit, or knew the abode, of that interesting canary.

One morning during the progress of this wearisome search—which had now begun to include even boarding-houses—the detective came across a little hostelry in South Boston, called the Warwick House. Somehow he had not met its name in the directories, nor had he thus far chanced on it in his diurnal promenades. He at once entered to make his customary inspection of the register, and found under the date of March 1st, an entry of " Chas. B. Wood and wife," New York.

Thomas gazed long and meditatively at the entry. Not only was this a date on which Dudley was stated to be in Boston, but there was a great resemblance in the handwriting to that of the many-named forger. These facts at once seemed to warrant a closer investigation.

"What day did my friend, Mr. Wood, leave?" in-quired Thomas, quite artlessly, of the young hotel-clerk—pointing him to the entry on the book.

"I can't say, sir," was the reply; "Mr. Fairbanks only became proprietor here on the fourth of the month, and the gentleman was not here then."

"Is the old porter around still?"

"No, sir, that's Patsey Clark,—he is now employed in the Eagle Livery Stables, which does the carriage service of the house."

With an impatient "Thank you" Mr. Thomas hastened out to the Eagle Livery stables, not far from the hotel.

Patsey Clark was not in; but the stable foreman was enabled to tell from his book that on the 7th of March a couple were taken from the Warwick House to the East-ern Railroad depot. The hack-driver was next found, and remembered the lady and gentleman, but couldn't describe them, and couldn't tell whether they had any baggage.

The persistent Thomas again went back to the War-wick House, and desired the clerk to tell him what gentleman had settled a bill for himself and lady on March 7th.

This time the clerk referred to his cash-book. "I beg pardon, it's here, sir," he said, "Chas. B. Wood and wife; but I really don't remember them—they must have settled with the proprietor."

"Will you please ask Mr. Fairbanks to step this way ?"

The proprietor soon came forth from a little parlor in rear of the hotel office.

"Do you remember this Mr. Wood and wife ?" now inquired Thomas, after a courteous greeting of Mr. Fairbanks.

"Yes,—pretty well," returned mine host of the Warwick.

"Well, I am almost certain he is a particular friend of mine, but I have forgotten Charley's full initials, and I never yet chanced to see his signature. Will you please describe Mr. and Mrs. Wood to me ?"

The obliging landlord put his finger thoughtfully to his brow, and proceeded to sketch from memory the appearance of his two recent guests. To the great interior gratification of Thomas, his descriptions were an exact reproduction of those graven on his own mind for Dudley and wife.

"Oh! thank you; that's my friend Wood, sure enough," exclaimed Thomas. "Did the party have a bird-cage with them ?—Charley's wife is very fond of canaries, and always takes her favorite along."

"It must be the same couple, sir," said Mr. Fairbanks; "I remember a bird-cage and a little square box going out with their trunks."

At this voluntary mention of what he believed must be the hat-box, the detective was in secret transports.

"Did Wood say where he was going, Mr. Fairbanks?"

"No, not to me, sir,—although I have an idea there was some mention of Portland, Maine. They went East, anyhow;—stay a moment—now I remember that Mr. Wood called in here a couple of weeks after; we merely saluted, however, for he only went to the bar and hurried out again."

"Greatly obliged, Mr. Fairbanks; good day, sir."

Thomas now hastened citywards to the telegraph office and apprised Mr. Linden of his latest discovery, and of his conviction that this Chas. B. Wood was Dudley beyond a doubt.

The astute Superintendent was not slow to perceive the true state of the case. Dudley was *not* in Boston after all, but was pretending to be, even to his own sister-in-law. As he had taken this Eastern Railroad, however, it was probable he had located somewhere on the line; and if not so far as Portland, Maine, then at some intermediate point, from which he was enabled to come to Boston occasionally to receive his Pittsburg letters. He now telegraphed Thomas his conclusions, with instructions to visit Portland first, and, if he met with no success there, to return at once in his tracks, and begin a systematic search in all the smaller towns from Lynn to Beverley.

In forty-eight hours from the receipt of this dispatch the detective had visited Portland, Maine, and scoured it from end to end without the least encouraging result. He next returned along the line,—of a Saturday morning it was,—and made a brief stop at Beverley. At that period it was quite a small place, without any hotels, so he contented himself with the positive assurance of the railroad station agent that no such persons or baggage had entered that village in several months. From Beverley he now crossed over to Salem, where traces were soon found which justified the belief that we had at last run Dudley to earth.

What these traces were we shall next see.

CHAPTER XXXI.

Sharp Skirmishing by Operative Thomas, with Landlords, Coach-men and Chambermaids.—He at last discovers a Mr. and Mrs. Goodhue, and a long-sought Canary-bird.

THE first proceeding of the detective at Salem was to interrogate the baggage-master, who proved to be a dull-witted and unaccommodating official. He knew nothing, recalled nothing, and apparently understood nothing.

Turning impatiently from him, Mr. Thomas next went to the Essex House, then the principal hotel in the ancient city. On the register there, he found under date of March 7th—that on which Wood left Boston—an entry of " H. Carter and wife, Room No. 6." Addressing himself to the landlord, who was present in the office, he made a polite inquiry about the personal appearance of Mr. and Mrs. Carter. The landlord either could not, or would not, remember anything about them ; and soon put a damper on Thomas's curiosity by the churlish announcement that "if parties came to stay at the Essex House, and paid their bills, they were never asked either for their photographs or their marriage certificates."

The detective now changed the subject quite pleasantly, and endeavored by a general conversation to win back the host into a more pliant humor. Apparently he succeeded in this; but on the subject of Carter and wife, the hotel-keeper continued to be provokingly forgetful. At length the conversation was interrupted by the return of the office-clerk, who had been out to his dinner, and Thomas noticed that as the landlord retired he whispered earnestly to his employee as if to warn him against the advances of the prying stranger.

To the other hotels in Salem the detective then betook himself, but at none of them found a trace of the object of his search. Some hours were consumed in traversing the long, elm-lined streets of the old peninsula; and as one of the hotels,—styled the Juniper House,—was at a distance of two miles from the

depot, the night had fallen heavily over Salem ere his
duty was completed.

But in all this time Mr. Thomas was thinking more
or less of his experience at the Essex House, and the
thought grew gradually into conviction, that the landlord of the hotel had something to conceal from him;
and that his hasty whisper to the clerk was a caution to
the same effect. There could be no doubt, he concluded, that even the porters would have been admon-
ished by this time; but he determined, notwithstanding, to return to the Essex, and there sojourn until the
mystery were cleared up.

As Mr. Thomas re-entered the hotel, he perceived
in the rear of the hall the porter seated on his bench.
With a new inspiration the detective immediately resolved on a bolder strategy. Without pausing at the
office, he advanced quickly towards where the man sat,
and promptly inquired of him :

"Do you remember that lady and gentleman with
the bird-cage, who came here about four weeks ago?"

The porter stammered, and then mumbled out a
reluctant "yes;" and then he added by way of qualifi-
cation :

"But I don't remember what they looked like, sir;
I only remember carrying the cage to No. 6."

Thomas had gained a point. There really was a
cage, then.

"Now try, like a good fellow," he continued, "if
12

you can't describe them to me a little ;—perhaps I may make it worth your while."

Thus tempted, the man seemed anxious to reply, but wavered and reddened as if constrained by fear, and looked out furtively in the direction of the office. At last he sought escape from his dilemma by saying that he thought the chambermaid might know better, and he would go and find her. Starting on the word he returned to Thomas in a very few moments, to say that the chambermaid knew nothing about any such people,—and as for himself, indeed, " he wasn't at all sure he was right."

Baffled, but not defeated, the detective walked back towards the desk, where he fancied he could notice in the landlord a look of vexation at his partial success with the porter. Thomas heeded it not, but stepped quickly out of doors, and in front of the adjoining stables found the driver of the hotel coach.

" Do you remember," he said to him, " the lady and gentleman with the bird-cage whom you took to the Essex a few weeks ago ?"

" I kinder recollects the cage," answered the driver " an' thet's abeout all I kin do. But neow theer's Hosee, the kerridge driver,—he might tell you jest what you want; he does a well-nigh all the kerridge work."

As he spoke he pointed to a hackman whose vehicle

stood at the neighboring corner, and who himself appeared a monopolist of his trade in Salem.

Thomas approached the man at once, but altered his question to meet the altered circumstances.

"Where did you drive that party with the bird-cage to?"

"What party?" returned Jehu, with characteristic gruffness.

"Why—that gentleman and lady that you took from the Essex House about four weeks ago."

"You mean the pair as hed two big trunks, band-box, two or three sachels, bird-cage, and a tarnation pile o' sich stuff?"

"Yes, that's the party;—where did you take them?"

"Wal, les see, I guess I took 'em to Mrs. Doyle's boardin'-house. Tall man, tall woman, wa'ant they?"

"Yes."

"They went down to Boston a few days ago, but didn't take no trunks along,"—now volunteered the hackman.

"Where is Mrs. Doyle's?" inquired Thomas.

"Thirty-three Summer Street," rejoined the man promptly, "air the folks friends o' yourn?"

"They are," said Thomas, "very old friends; thank you."

Putting a dollar bill into the hackman's willing

fingers, the officer turned back in the direction of the hotel.

"You're putty sartin to find 'em at Doyle's," the accommodating personage shouted after him.

There being no trains for Boston on the Sunday, Mr. Thomas deferred all further action until Monday. Bright and early on that day he was at No. 33 Summer Street, inquiring of Mrs. Doyle with engaging simplicity for "that gentleman and wife, Mr.—Mr.—hem, —the couple that came to board with her about four weeks ago; Mr.—how *was* it that the name escaped him so ?"

"Oh, you mean Mr. Goodhue, sir ?"

"Yes, thank you; I believe that's the name,—what kind of looking man was he."

"He was a tall man, sir,—a little taller than you, dark complexion;—very nice people both."

"Did they bring their baggage here, Mrs. Doyle ?"

"They did, sir, but they only stayed a short while —they were out most of the time looking for a house and furnishing it."

"Yes, it must be the same," said the detective approvingly; "if they be the persons I expect, Mrs. Doyle, they are dear old friends of mine, and will be greatly pleased, as well as surprised, to see me. Where did they take up house, please ?"

"Well, I believe they are living at No. 396 Essex Street," answered the obliging lady.

The detective beheld a sheeny yellow cage with a pretty canary bird.

" Thank you;—they'll be so glad to see me!— good morning, Mrs. Doyle," said Thomas, and then hastened towards Essex Street, feeling as he went along as if the arrest warrant for Dudley was safe in his pocket, and his man as good as already captured.

In Essex Street, at the number indicated, a tidy-looking housemaid had just begun opening the parlor lattice blinds. Without ascending the stoop the detective addressed her:

" Is Mr. Goodhue within, please?"

" No, sir," replied the girl, "he is out of town, and we don't expect him home before Wednesday."

" So long as that!" exclaimed the crestfallen Thomas, as if he were impatient to greet the absent Goodhue,—which in good truth he was.

" I think so," explained the housemaid, civilly, " for Mrs. Goodhue is sick abed, but I wrote him this morning that she was much better, and that he need not hurry home."

" Is it a friend?" she inquired of Thomas, as she proceeded to unfasten the blind of the other window.

" Yes, thank you; but I'll call another day—good-morning."

Before he walked away, however, the remaining blind was thrown back; and there, hanging square in the window, between the drooping lace curtains, the detective beheld a sheeny yellow cage with a pretty canary-bird! As the April sunshine glinted on its prison bars, the bird warbled out its blithe matin song; and Thomas paused awhile to listen, and to chirrup to it caressingly, as if he would coax from its little melodies the secret of its owner. At all events he seemed to discern in them the notes of his own triumph ; and as he left the place, looked back upon the dainty songster as a kind of hostage for Dudley's return.

Nor did the delay until Wednesday now seem irksome, as he rambled hopefully through the Salem streets, whistling and trilling to every song-bird he could find. It was an interval which added one more to the many acquirements of our Operative, who became at Salem a most expert warbler,—or, if the barbarism may pass, a kind of human mocking-bird !

CHAPTER XXXII.

Detective Thomas is provided with an assistant.—Discomfiture,
Delays and fresh Disappointments.

IT seemed to Detective Thomas almost a heresy to doubt that Messrs. Wood, of the Warwick House ; Carter, of the Essex ; and Goodhue who made his home in Salem, were but a single individual, and that individual the fugitive Dudley. The date of Wood's departure from Boston, and of Carter's appearance in Salem ; the personal descriptions of the two parties ; the concealment aimed at by the landlord of the Essex ; the setting-up house under the fictitious name of Goodhue ; and last, but not least, the similarity of baggage—down even to the canary and its yellow cage—all seemed to point to the correctness of this deduction.

At this very period Mr. Linden had begun to fear that Thomas, unaided, would scarcely succeed in finding Dudley in Boston. He had never in his life laid eyes upon the forger, either in the flesh, or in his picture. His only means of a personal recognition was the study he had made of the written descriptions furnished to him. And, illusory as such portraitures often are, and easy as it would be for Dudley to disguise himself, it was evident that the swindler might pass Thomas in the street, and excite no suspicion unless specially brought to notice.

On this unpleasant hypothesis the Superintendent had requested Mr. Loomis, of Pittsburg, to spend a few days with our detective in Boston. As Loomis knew thoroughly well the personal appearance of the forger, the latter certainly couldn't escape them if he ventured into public places,—the design being that they should visit these as frequently as possible, and perambulate the streets from day's dawn to midnight in the hope to fall in with Dudley.

When the encouraging news from Salem reached

Philadelphia, Loomis had just arrived in that city, bearing with him a warrant for the arrest of Dudley and wife, obtained in Pittsburg by the Agent of Adams' Express. When he reported at the Agency Mr. Linden apprised him of the new aspect of affairs, and requested him to go right through to Salem to identify the forger in the person of Goodhue.

Having arranged to be absent from his own business for a vacation, the insurance agent consented to adopt any requisite course. Mr. Thomas was now advised by telegraph of the ally that was coming to his assistance, and instructed to provide Loomis with an opportunity to identify Goodhue as soon as possible after the return of the latter. While arranging for this encounter the Pittsburger was to remain carefully in the background, or else reasonably disguised, so that Dudley should not recognize him and take flight before the officer was on hand to capture him.

In the forenoon of the day that was to bring back to Salem the owner of the canary-bird, Loomis arrived there, and joined Mr. Thomas at his hotel, as he had formerly done in Yarmouth. As prearranged by the careful Superintendent they did not recognize each other until they were out of doors and free from observation. All that morning the detective had been watching No. 396 Essex Street, but saw no sign of the return of its tenant, nor any indication that there was a man on the premises. Expectation having been pitched high the circumstance occasioned a corresponding uneasiness. Did Goodhue—that is, Dudley,—mean to return at all?—had anybody given the alarm since Monday?—or, was that surly, ungracious landlord of the Essex in his counsels, and had he telegraphed him a warning that pursuers were on hand? Such were the doubts that had agitated Mr. Thomas.

The officer and Mr. Loomis together now continued till nightfall watching the incoming trains; but none of them brought to Salem the person of the forger. After dark they ventured out to Essex Street to take a survey of the house, but to all appearance it had no other occupants than the servant and her sick mistress. Plainly enough, then, Mr. Goodhue had not yet returned, and the patience of Thomas must be strained through another night.

In the morning, after an early breakfast, the two again proceeded to Essex Street, and called in at a grocery store nearly opposite Goodhue's house, with the object of discovering if that person were returned home. To gain a little time for their survey Thomas bought cigars, and the two continued smoking in the store, and chatting with the grocer and his clerk.

While they were thus engaged the door of No. 396 opened, and a gentleman in slippers came out, and crossed over the street in the direction of the grocery. He carried a little wicker basket in his hand, and had evidently—like a kind, domesticated citizen,—come

12*

forth for some necessaries for the morning meal of his household. As he passed in, unheeding, by the two smokers, and stepped up to the counter, the grocer saluted him as an esteemed customer.

" Good morning, Mr. Goodhue!—I see you're got back to town ; what can I do for you this morning, sir ?"

Thomas looked towards Loomis in grim anticipation. Loomis walked around and about, and peered from every point on the face of the Salemite. Quite unconcernedly that gentleman bought his fresh eggs, and rolls, and other breakfast ingredients ; and then, resuming his little basket, went back to the house. Loomis was shaking his head negatively.

" Is that the Mr. Goodhue who took a house round here a few weeks ago?" inquired Thomas of the grocer.

" That's the gentleman, sir ; he bought that house over the way, No. 396 ;—there where you see the canary cage,—that's his house."

" Thank you, sir ; good morning."

The disgusted and impatient Thomas then led the way into the street.

" So that's not Dudley ?" he demanded, turning to his companion the moment they were beyond earshot.

" No," answered the latter, " not Dudley,—though like him in a way."

" Quite sure there's no mistake, now ?"

"Oh! most positive," reiterated Loomis; "I couldn't be mistaken about Dudley;—besides, that man is several years older than he is."

Thomas would not be satisfied, however. His friend might have forgotten—he might have been thinking of some one else,—the man's whiskers had grown,—his accent was perhaps feigned,—in short, there were so many very excellent reasons why Goodhue must be Dudley, that—that—really Mr. Loomis must be so kind as go and speak with him, and have another good, square, convincing look at him.

It was then arranged for the insurance man to call at once at Goodhue's, and engage that person in conversation about a house next door which chanced to be for rent. If he saw any grounds for revising his previous judgment, and coming to the conclusion that he had found the forger, a signal was agreed on which would bring Thomas to his side in a moment. The latter took post in the street near by, chafing with impatience, and fretted beyond measure by repeated discomfiture and delays.

On ringing at the door of No. 396, it was Goodhue himself who answered the bell; and without any show of reluctance or trepidation he held civil converse with the pretended house-hunter for a space of several minutes.

Once more the Pittsburger rejoined Mr. Thomas, and shaking his head determinedly :—

' That's not Dudley," he repeated.

Within an hour from this singular and provoking misadventure, the detective and his companion took their leave of Salem. At Lynn, the village pearl of Massachusetts Bay, they made a fresh pause and a fresh search; but nothing resulted except fresh disappointment. Early in the afternoon they were at dinner together in Boston, apparently as far from success as ever.

But our officer had no leisure to mope over his reverses. Immediately after the meal he took Mr. Loomis out with him, and they proceeded without delay to the Warwick House, in South Boston, to inquire of its proprietor if Mr. and Mrs. Wood had again passed that way. The supposition was now reasonable, that Mr. Carter, alias Goodhue, of Salem, was not the same individual who left the Warwick House to go East on the 7th of March. That the latter, however, was Dudley was an opinion to which Thomas still adhered with tenacity. The Salemite he had now mentally consigned to the limbo of mistaken identities.

The views of the detective were confirmed by a fresh description of his late guest, obligingly given by Mr. Fairbanks; and which satisfied even Loomis that Chas. B. Wood was the real Simon Pure. But, alas! where was Wood? He had not since vouchsafed to repeat his visits to the Warwick House; and the last glimpse obtained of him was in that hasty call at the bar-room, three weeks before. So affirmed Mr. Fair-banks.

The searchers began now their grand exploration of the city, on the chance to encounter Dudley at large in some of its promenades. It being the first day of May the weather was delicious,—a perfect "bridal of the earth and sky,"—and staid old Boston seemed all out-of-doors, making merry in the Spring sunshine. Surely this Dudley would for once be tempted from his re-treat! Surely he was not all so criminal and heart-jaded that he could resist the witchery of the lovely vernal season!

And so, each taking a side-walk, and advancing somewhat abreast, the detective and his companion threaded their way watchfully among the circulating thousands of Boston. Any one at all conforming to the general outline of Dudley, became, for either or both, the object of a hurried scrutiny. If Thomas got the impression that he recognized him in some passing citizen, he would summon Loomis to his side to verify or correct,—but invariably the latter, as it this day chanced. If Loomis noticed a pedestrian with some feature of close resemblance to Dudley, he would call Thomas to remark it, that henceforth he might asso-ciate it with the forger himself. And thus it came to pass, that with the nose and chin of one Bostonian, the eyes and mouth of another, and the figure, gait, or general style of others, the detective had constructed for him a fresh portrait of Dudley, which was at least an improvement on what he had conceived from the written descriptions.

In this way the hours were passed until sundown, but neither in street, nor square, nor promenade, nor in the beautiful Boston Common,—which that day was thronged with legions of gay New Englanders,—could a glimpse be obtained of the object of such keen solicitude.

After supper there was no better success, although the audiences of two or three theatres were included among the crowds inspected.

CHAPTER XXXIII.

A Deadlock all Around.—Mrs. Pelham's little Scheme to induce Lizzie Greenleaf to accompany her to Boston, proves a Failure.

IN Pittsburg meanwhile Mrs. Pelham continued to intrigue, and Delaney to shadow. For the detective, each passing day was now but a repetition of the preceding one. There was so little in the movements of Miss Greenleaf that was out of the regular routine, that the detective's duty was monotonous and unfruitful. That she still maintained a correspondence with her sister in New England, was placed beyond doubt by her own averments. But aside from the fact that she had twice put letters into a street postal-box, Delaney could acquire no knowledge whatever of this correspondence. One stolen glance at an envelope would have given him the precious secret; but no such chance seemed likely to happen.

Mrs. Pelham, as we have seen, was scarcely more successful. In every conversation with Lizzie the latter had continued to be as guarded of Dudley's address as she was in her terse communication to Wales. The lady, in short, was making no progress whatever.

Thus, taking into account the part of Mr. Thomas in the operation, there seemed to be a kind of deadlock all around ; and this was far from being pleasant either to the Agency or to the Express Company,—to us, because we held a prisoner unarraigned; to them, because of the expense that was accumulating at Boston and Pittsburg.

But with all this our female detective was still looked upon as a sound reliance. The demeanor of Lizzie Greenleaf had not visibly changed towards her ; and to all appearance the girl was unsuspicious of a snare. If their intimacy could only advance as it had grown up, the acquisition of the secret was but a question of time. That it should not become chilled, or be disrupted, was the care of the General Superintendent.

In this view Mr. Bangs had now supplied Mrs. Pelham with letters of introduction to some prominent citizens of Pittsburg, ostensibly to facilitate her start in business. If the delay or non-execution of this project should occasion any surprise to Lizzie, the display of such letters would at least prevent mistrust. For the girl to feel satisfied that her new-made friend was acting in good faith, was of all things essential to the growth of their friendly relations.

And sure enough the cautious young damsel inquired of the lady if she had furnished herself with such letters. It was so reasonable that a person should do so who contemplated a business venture in a strange city, that the question came up very naturally in one of their conferences about the new store. It was answered with a ready affirmative, and in a matter-of-fact way ; and the perusal soon after of some of the letters themselves, seemed to remove from Lizzie a cloud of gathering doubt. At all events she displayed less of reserve in her general intercourse, and became as frank and companionable as opportunity at all permitted.

But there was just the rub. Opportunity did not permit much. Their interviews in Dunstable's store were limited as to time, and for obvious reasons greatly constrained. Her sister, Mrs. Marsh, was now dangerously ill, too, and most of the girl's spare hours were absorbed in visits to her house. At the solicitation of Lizzie herself, Mrs Pelham had even begun to attend at the same place of worship with her, but still without adding to the facilities for free intercourse. Herself and Lizzie now enjoyed the same magazines and books; consulted each other's tastes in affairs of dress; and pondered together the news-topics of the day; but all without attaining to the end we had in view. Lizzie spoke no more of Etta and her husband; Mrs. Pelham feared to broach the subject, or found no suitable occasion.

To make a finish of this "masterly inactivity," I now suggested to Bangs that our lady detective should in some way persuade Miss Greenleaf to make a flying visit to Boston with her, she paying the double expenses as an inducement to the girl. The Superintendent wrought out this idea fully in a letter of instructions to Mrs. Pelham; and to get over her unacquaintance with the city,—for, in sooth, she had never been there,—he arranged to have a detective meet them and officiate as her "cousin" and escort. Delaney was to follow closely if the ladies left Pittsburg; and to shadow Lizzie in Boston until she came in contact with the Dudleys.

The morning after she had received these instructions Mrs. Pelham called at the store, with the momentous purpose of buying a pair of gloves.

"Are you going out at noon-time to-day?" she inquired of Miss Greenleaf, while the latter was stretching the gloves for her.

"Yes," replied Lizzie, "I am going to my sister's in

Alleghany City; Grandma is there this morning, and I have promised I would meet her."

"Oh! that's really too bad," exclaimed Mrs. Pelham, "I was in hopes you would be disengaged, as I had some business matters to talk to you about;—I must wait, I suppose, until you are more at liberty."

"Business!" repeated the girl, with manifest interests, "you can say what you please right here,—no one will interrupt us."

"Well, I simply want to know can you get a leave of absence from the store?"

"How?—for an hour or two, is it?"

"Oh! more than that;—I mean for a week or two."

"Quite impossible," returned Lizzie, in a decided manner; "why, we are only just getting into the busy season, and absence is out of the question until the regular vacation time, last of July, or beginning of August;—we all get a week's rest about then."

"Dear me! I am sorry," said the lady, in a tone of disappointment; "I wanted you so much to go East with me to select a stock of goods."

"What!" exclaimed Miss Greenleaf, her face all aglow with satisfaction; "would you trust me to buy a stock of goods for you?"

"I certainly should," was the answer; "I have observed you quite closely, and I feel sure that with what I know myself, and your experience in the requirements of a western trade, we could select a very salable invoice."

Lizzie laughed pleasantly.

"I am altogether too little," she said, "for such a big responsibility."

"Nevertheless, I would trust you entirely," repeated Mrs. Pelham.

The compliment seemed very agreeable to the young clerk, who now inquired if Mrs. Pelham had at last decided to go into business in Pittsburg.

"Oh! yes, that's about settled," replied the lady; "but the goods I want now are not for my own business, but for a store in Iowa belonging to a cousin of mine. Hitherto, either himself or his partner always went East in the season, but he writes me that he is quite indisposed, and that his partner is at present away from the store. He wishes me to go to New York and Boston to get the Spring stock for him,—indeed, he says it should now be on the way, the season is so advanced. Well, you know, of myself, Miss Greenleaf, I have not sufficient experience to determine all his wants," concluded Mrs. Pelham, "and thinking of your desire to go to Boston, it seemed a capital piece of management to get you along with me."

"I am greatly flattered and obliged, indeed," observed Lizzie, regretfully, "and I would certainly go if it were at all possible. But why not buy here, Mrs.

Pelham ?—we have a large stock of goods and will sell you very low."

" That may be," said the lady, "but still you must have your commissions on them ; and I know I could do better in the large wholesale houses of B ston,— particularly as I have some friends there. I am sure that with your assistance I could have saved enough on the trip to pay your expenses and lost time ;—you see I am nearly half way from Iowa, and if Mr. Kelly has to go himself he will have twice the distance to travel."

" I'm so sorry," renewed Lizzie ; "but you are not very strong yourself, Mrs. Pelham,—I don't think you should undertake such a fatiguing journey."

" I have been so entreated," answered that lady, re-signedly, "that I can scarcely see how to get out of it. It depends on how I feel, though ;—I may still tele-graph my cousin that I cannot possibly go for him."

The conversation now touched on other matters, and momentarily on Mrs. Marsh's health, of which Lizzie stated that there was a great improvement, but that the lady was not yet out of danger.

" It's just my luck," added the girl, pettishly ; "I don't expect anything else but that when my vacation comes round, she will be so sick that I cannot get to Boston."

" You have written your other sister then, that you are going to visit her during vacation ?"

'I have; although Grandma says I must not go. It is so long since we have lived together that she wants to keep me to herself all summer."

" Gracious !—you may not go at all, then ?"

" Yes, indeed I shall," said Lizzie, with pouting emphasis; " I have never been to Boston yet, and I want to see it above all things;—it will be so very pleasant now that sister is keeping house for herself."

Nothing else material to our narrative transpired at this interview; except perhaps a statement of Miss Greenleaf that if her sister continued better she would leave town for her grandmother's house within the coming week. Her refusal to accompany Mrs. Pelham to Boston was just one more defeat in our attempts to track Dudley to his lair.

Succeeding this were two or three other meetings, in which the allusions made by Lizzie to her absent sister were deplorably brief and unsatisfying. Although seemingly as cordial as ever, she avoided this subject as if by design; and when impelled to it by hint or question, her replies were as vague as they could well be framed, and a fresh topic was clutched at with manifest relief.

Just here, too, came in a phenomenon, which might be better accounted for by a pathologist than a detective. The clever and energetic lady who had sustained this intercourse with Lizzie, adroit and self-possessed as she continued to be in her presence, was greatly unstrung by the failure of all her devices. So intense had been the strain on her mental resources, and so high-wrought the hopes thus baffled at every point, that she became subject when alone to the most distressing sensations. Apprehensive of every shadow on the path of her advance, she could not help fancying —and especially when Lizzie would turn upon her those large magnetic eyes—that the girl had penetrated her real object, and was pretending to a confidence she was far from feeling.

Mrs. Pelham, in short, was sick of unsuccess.

CHAPTER XXXIV.

Mrs. Pelham, the Shrewd Lady Detective, endeavors to further Ensnare Miss Lizzie Greenleaf, and though beaten by that quite as shrewd little Individual at every Point, still retains the latter's Confidence.

MISS GREENLEAF was now several days absent from the store. No clue to the actual cause was discovered by Delaney, until Mrs. Pelham had learned at Dunstable's that Lizzie was ill. During this period of enforced inaction Mrs. Pelham was literally on the rack,—filled with anxiety for her mission and burning with impatience at its failure of results. A multitude of new schemes for obtaining the forger's address were hourly revolved in her brain, and with those which had been suggested by Mr. Bangs, rehearsed to happy issue in the silent chambers of her thoughts. To put some of them to test on the very first opportunity at length became her firm and pervading purpose.

The occasion was not very long in presenting itself. Going into Dunstable's one morning at ten o'clock, she found to her relief that Lizzie was again at her post. The girl appeared much pleased at the visit; and explained her absence by stating that she had suffered from a spell of neuralgic face-ache,—of which, indeed, the traces were yet visible. Her sister's health was also spoken of, and her sufferings in a perilous crisis feelingly recounted.

Mrs. Pelham now fell back on the usual shopping pretext, and requested to be shown some heavy vails and then some traveling gloves, in both of which articles she made an investment. While thus engaged she asked Lizzie if she would not call on her in the hotel at noon-time.

The girl replied that she had brought her dinner with her and did not intend leaving the store that day.

In the interval of restraint which followed, the detective felt as if at her wits' end; but with the latest communication from Bangs fresh in her memory, she resolved on a supreme effort to satisfy his urgency. The lace counter happened to be just then unoccupied, and moving that way she begged Lizzie to show her down some laces she had been examining on a previous occasion. While they were occupied in comparing the different patterns she observed to the young girl:

"I am so glad to have found you at the store this morning, for I am going out of town, and feared I might not see you again."

Lizzie looked up at her with unfeigned concern.

"Going!" she exclaimed; "where to? I did think rather strange of your getting those gloves, and that thick vail; but it never once occurred to me that you were going to leave the city."

"I am sorry it must be so," said Mrs. Pelham, "but my cousin is quite sick, and thinks it better for me to go East for him,—even if I must go alone."

"And so you are really going?"

"Yes; I must go to-morrow morning—although to tell the truth I don't feel quite strong enough to make the journey at present. I have just sent a final dispatch to Mr. Kelly, to induce him, if possible, to order his goods through the commission house,—but I have no idea that he will purchase in that way."

Mrs. Pelham here took out her pocket-book, and extracting from it a card and pencil, said:

"Now, Miss Greenleaf, if you will give me your sister's address I will make an effort to call on her while in Boston."

The lady looked straight into Lizzie's face as she

waited for the pregnant answer. With supreme composure the young girl replied :

"I would with pleasure, but I don't know where she is."

"What?—you don't know where your sister is ?"

"No ; I know she is in Boston, but I don't know in what part."

"You don't know the street and number then ?"

"I do not, indeed ;—I only heard once from her since she went to Boston, and then they were on the point of going to housekeeping."

"How can you direct your letters, if not ?"

"Sister Etta told me to address her simply to Boston, Massachusetts.

"My goodness !—I should think it strange if such letters would ever reach her in so large a city," observed the lady.

"I suppose it is," responded Lizzie, in a meek, undemonstrative way.

"Then if you had gone to Boston with me you couldn't have found her ?"

"Oh ! yes, I should ; in that case I'd have written to her first, and Etta would be sure to come meet me."

Thus far Mrs. Pelham had been utterly worsted, but like a good general she decided to retreat with her face to the enemy.

"Have you told her," she now inquired, unaffectedly, "that your other sister was so very sick ?"

13

"Not yet," replied Lizzie; "I have been expecting every day to get a letter from her, and shall not tell her till I do."

"I am always on my stepping stones," she added, with assumed stateliness, "if I do not hear from Etta just about so often."

"Well," said the tranquil Mrs. Pelham, "I am really disappointed;—I should so like to have seen the sister who resembles you so closely as you say she does."

"I am sorry I can't help it," said the girl; "I wish I could tell you where she lives."

Mrs. Pelham had now selected the lace, and after looking into her purse, exclaimed:

"How very provoking to be sure! I have been so flurried about leaving town that I didn't think of having to buy this lace to-day,—but I have no intention of letting that pretty pattern be lost. Now, Miss Greenleaf, if I take it will you bring it over to the Diamond at noontime, and have some dinner with me, and I shall pay you for it there. Ever since I came to Pittsburg I have made it a practice not to carry much money with me in the streets."

"I can send the boy over with it," suggested the distracting Lizzie.

"No, no; that won't do;—I must see you once more before I leave the city."

"Well, well, I'll come over," said Lizzie with

a laugh,—"that is, if nobody elopes with me in the meanwhile."

Mrs. Pelham now returned to the hotel. Her attempt to surprise from Lizzie the whereabouts of her brother-in-law had failed like the rest; but she was by no means yet at the end of her resources. So long as she was not actually discovered, and could see and speak with the girl at all, the chances of success were still worth depending on. Nor had there been anything in the morning's conversation,—exceptional as it was,—to indicate on the part of Lizzie a waning trust, or a doubt that her customer was in all respects truthful. Either the girl really did not, as she had stated, know of her sister's exact address; or it was the one reservation on which she was guarded against every approach.

The first thing, then, for Mrs. Pelham to do, was *not* to go away from Pittsburg. This she readily arranged. From a number of blank telegraph forms, with which she had been supplied by Mr. Bangs, she selected one of those used for a message received. On this she wrote in a clerkly hand a dispatch to herself, as if coming from her Iowa cousin, Mr. Kelly; and with the envelope of an old telegram threw it carelessly on the dressing-table in her room. While at the store with Lizzie she had held in her hand a letter just received from the Agency, of which she knew that the postmark had not been exposed. For this she seemed

to have other use ; and laid it on the window-sill beside which she usually seated herself. She then sat
down to wait,—despairing of success, yet desperate of
intent.

The noon dinner-hour had in great part expired
when Lizzie came in with the little parcel of lace. To
her amazement, her friend was crying bitterly, while
her face showed the traces of abundant weeping.

" Why—Mrs.—Pelham ! what *ever* can be the matter with you ? have you heard bad news ?"

" Oh ! Miss Greenleaf—I little dreamed—" sobbed
out the lady, between her spasms of grief, " I little
knew what a source of wretchedness I carried in my
hand from the post-office this sad morning. It is only
since I came in that I got a chance—that I managed
to read—that long letter from my sister"—here she
indicated the letter on the window-sill—" and ah ! she
is in such sad trouble, indeed. Do, pray excuse me, Miss
Greenleaf, for I—I'm—so overwhelmed—so—"

" What has happened to her ?" inquired the girl, in
tones of friendly anxiety. " Is she sick,—has she been
hurt ?"

" No, no, no," exclaimed the weeping woman, " but
I dare not speak of it—of her afflictions—eagerly as I
crave for sympathy at such a moment."

" Really, dear Mrs. Pelham," said the good-hearted
girl, " I feel very, very sorry to see you in such distress."

" Thank you, dear child, thank you ; you are the

"Why, Mrs. Pelham! what ever can be the matter?"

only soul in Pittsburg in whom I have one particle of trust. I know it would do me good to tell you—but, oh!—" here there was a fresh paroxysm of tearful lamentation—"but you must not speak of it—you must not reveal to any one—the world is so very censorious—it might ruin the prospects of the little business I hope to establish."

"I am sure," said Lizzie, whose womanly curiosity had now become excited, "I am certain, Mrs. Pelham, that you may rely on my friendship and discretion. I never speak of that which is confided to me in trust."

Mrs. Pelham knew it, indeed, but too well.

It was only, however, after another interval of sobs and tears, and sympathetic assurances from Lizzie, that the lady managed to falter out that her poor sister, Mrs. White, had a good husband, a very good husband indeed, but he was lately in such terrible trouble that she often found herself wishing that her sister had no husband at all!

"Indeed, the world might be all the better if a good many of the husbands were dead and out of it," interposed the philosophic young maiden.

But Mrs. Pelham struggled bravely on, and informed Lizzie how Mrs. White was almost insane over the disgrace of her chosen partner. He had been a stock speculator, she said, and a few months before had bought some Union Pacific bonds, and sold them again, and they turned out to be forgeries;—Mr. White, of course being ignorant of the last dreadful fact. But notwithstanding his innocence, he had been followed all over the country by *them*—the meanest of all created beings—Pinkerton's detectives, and at last they had caught him, and were holding him in jail at Cleveland, Ohio.

Lizzie here stamped her little foot on the floor, and gave vent to the opinion that there was "nothing in the world too vile for the same despicable crew,—those detectives would hire out their very souls, and swear just as they were ordered, without the least regard for truth!"

This sweeping denunciation of the Pinkerton people served to gratify and console the sorrowing Mrs. Pelham; who now gave further details—and most pathetically—of the misfortunes of the White family.

Her young Pittsburg friend listened to them with the gravest concern, once expressing as her principle that "she would never go back on a friend because he had got into trouble!" She also charitably administered such consolation as she could think of, until she had brought Mrs. Pelham into a more tranquil frame of mind.

"If Mr. White," she observed towards the end, "if your brother-in-law can only employ good counsel, you may be sure he will come out all right from his trouble."

For this, and other such sisterly assurances, Mrs. Pelham was, of course, quite profuse in her thanks.

But in all this affecting scene, with its yearning grief and heart-wrung disclosures, the wily little maiden spake not one word of Etta and her husband. The skeleton in her friend's closet had been unvailed to her without stint; but, contrary to all feminine example, she did not reciprocate by laying bare that which was locked within her own.

When sufficiently composed to do so Mrs. Pelham paid Lizzie for the lace, and begged her to stay and take dinner with her; but this the girl declined on the plea of having lunched at the store.

With a sigh of martyr-like resignation, the lady then rang to have her own dinner brought to the room; whereupon Lizzie started up to go, first turning towards the dressing-table to arrange her hat,—a movement which, with consummate knowledge of her sex, Mrs. Pelham had correctly anticipated. The telegram so carefully —yet carelessly—displayed, of course caught her eye.

"Oh! you have got a dispatch?" she inquired.

"Yes, dear," replied Mrs. Pelham, with a faint smile of returning animation, "just a little before you came in;—you will see it is from Cousin Kelly, who at last consents to manage his purchases through some eastern commission house."

Lizzie did take a glance at the telegram, and appeared much pleased that such was its purport.

"Oh! I am glad," she said; "it would be harder than ever for you to go East just at present."

Shortly afterwards she went out, Mrs. Pelham seeing her to the head of the staircase. That lady then returned to her room, and after removing the last traces of her recent grief, sat down to her little *menu* of salmon and green peas, with a degree of composure quite remarkable under the circumstances. She smiled even at the thought, that if she had failed in her demand for Etta's address, she had also most effectually destroyed any suspicion that might have attached to it.

She dined heartily; and on her sunny face there was no longer any traces of grief for the sorrows of her mythical sister.

CHAPTER XXXV.

Miss Greenleaf herself turns Detective and asks Leading Questions.—A Notable Interview.—A curious Change in Dunstable & Co.'s Clerk —No further Traces of the Forger.

TO sustain the fiction used by our lady Operative, Mr. Linden now inclosed a letter to a friend in Cleveland, to be immediately remailed to Mrs. Pelham, at Pittsburg. The letter purported to be from Mrs. White to her "dearest sister," thanking her exuberantly for the comfort conveyed in some imaginary communication, and continuing the gloomy record of her own troubles. The design of it simply was, that it might be opportunely shown to Lizzie, and reassure her

thoroughly as to Mrs. Pelham's truthfulness, as well as
engage all her sympathies for a friend whose family
associations were so distressingly like her own.

The necessity for just such credentials had meanwhile been made painfully apparent at the very theatre
of action. It was several days subsequent to the
episode at the Diamond Hotel before Mrs. Pelham again
met Lizzie at Dunstable's store. In the interval, however,—and indeed on the very day after,—Delaney
had observed the girl reading a letter with deep attention, as she walked back from Alleghany City after a
noon visit at her sister's.

On this occasion, when Mrs. Pelham called, Lizzie
received her with unusual warmth, and explained to
her how the illness of her other sister, Mrs. Stacey, had
detained her a couple of days at her Auntie's house.
Various other topics were then discoursed about,
when the girl interposed quite voluntarily:

" What do you think, Mrs. Pelham,—my visit to
Boston will have to be given up !"

" What !—given up ?" returned the astonished lady.

" Yes," explained the girl; "I have had a letter
from sister Etta, and they are gone to New York !"

Mrs. Pelham became anxious—and also suspicious.

" Have they left Boston for good ?" she placidly
inquired.

" It seems so," said Lizzie, " they got tired of it, or
rather he did, and now they are in New York. They

13*

don't exactly know, either, where they will go next ;—
he is never very long contented anywhere."

"Of course they have friends in New York ?" pursued the detective.

"Oh! yes; but I doubt not they are at a hotel,—
sister didn't exactly say ; but she did say she was very
tired of traveling all the time, and would come to stay
with me a while during the summer,—though she dis-
likes Pittsburg so much that I hardly think she will
stay very long."

"When did you hear of this change from her ?'
was next inquired, with seeming unconcern.

"Two or three mornings ago,—I forget which,—·
I know they wrote on the first. Goodness knows where
they will be next time they write ;—they are always
flitting about so."

"Well, if his business is traveling I suppose they
can't well do otherwise," serenely observed Mrs. Pelham.

"True, but he might go into some other business,"
rejoined the girl.

"Why don't you send him a good scold of a letter,
then ?"

"Indeed," said Lizzie, with a show of petulance,
"I shan't write to Etta for weeks now, just because she
has kept me waiting so long this time."

A turn now came in the conversation, some trifling
purchases were made, and some time expended in im-
material gossip. Once more the spell was broken by

Lizzie, who almost startled Mrs. Pelham by the oddity of her questions.

" Do you know a man named Harry Norman ?" was the singular inquiry.

The lady had heard the question very distinctly, but to get her thoughts well under control she pretended not.

" What did you say ?" she returned.

" Did you ever meet a Mr. Norman when you were in New York ?"

" Norman ?—Norman ?—" echoed Mrs. Pelham, reflectively.

" Yes ; his first name was Harry."

" Well, it does seem to me—I imagine I have known some one by that name ;—I think it was the name of a gentleman whom I once met at a New York hotel ;—he was a drummer for a dry-goods house. Was that your friend's business ?"

" Oh ! he is not my friend," replied Lizzie, quickly ; only I met him about two years ago."

" Harry Norman is a pretty name," observed Mrs. Pelham.

" Yes, and he is a real pleasant fellow," asserted Lizzie.

" The more I think of it the more I believe that the person *I* met was called Norwood, said the lady ;— " but still it may have been the same. What kind of looking man is he ?"

" Rather good looking," answered Lizzie ; " I think

he has a light moustache. Have you ever seen a Mr. Wales ?"

"Wales !" exclaimed the lady, who at this point could scarce have been startled at anything; "what a queer name that is, to be sure."

"Yes, I think so too."

Looking her catechist soberly in the face Mrs. Pelham gave the reply that she "never remembered hearing the name except as a country in geographies. "

"That's so," rejoined Lizzie, with a light metallic laugh that struck unpleasantly on the ears of the anxious detective.

"Are they friends of your brother-in-law ?" now ventured the latter.

"No, no ; not at all."

"Oh! I thought you might have met them while visiting your sister in New York ?"

"No, " repeated Lizzie, "I met them while they were here in Pittsburg."

"What business is Mr. Wales engaged in ?"

At this question Lizzie flushed somewhat; then laughed a little, and said : "I don't really know. I believe they are generally in New York : anyhow I know they are there often."

This fitful conversation took still another turn, during which Lizzie once remarked, and again without any prompting :

"Well, I am not so sorry after all that Etta has left

Boston, for they might now stay in New York, and I should just as soon visit them there."

This notable interview was soon after terminated, and the first step of the bewildered Mrs. Pelham was to telegraph the Agency that Lizzie had asserted Dudley to be in New York on the first of May,—the very day on which Thomas and his friend began their weary search for him in the highways and byways of Boston. Mr. Bangs was very much surprised, and at once sent out his officers to scour the Empire City; but when, on the morrow, Mrs. Pelham's full report of the conversation was received, his surprise not only vanished, but gave place to downright incredulity.

"Very remarkable interview, indeed," he soliloquized, scanning the report for the second or third time; "quite a sensation from the start. Greeted her with unusual warmth, the lady says;—evidently the little puss had an object in view, and what could it be, if not to impress on her friend the sacred intimacy that bound them? Here, too, she talks of the Dudleys, all in a spasm,—as if she must tell the news or burst! Very curious change in Miss Greenleaf, who has always had to be pressed hard to touch on the subject at all. Yes, and she talks copiously; emphasizes by repetition the statement that her sister is in New York; hastens to account for it by saying Dudley got tired of Boston; —and how very eagerly she does it all—how anxious she is to be believed! Pshaw! her very eagerness defeats her own purpose. Strange thing it would be for a man to tire of a city, who had only been a few days in it, and all the time busied in preparing himself a new home! And then, she says not a word of sister Etta's desolation at the collapse of her first housekeeping experiment. How easy both sisters take it, to be sure! Only two weeks ago a fixture in Boston, and now, a disrupted home, a hasty flight to New York, and heaven knows where beyond, and not one word of sisterly regret, even to her bosom friend! And there's the abandonment of her own trip East,—so unconcernedly, so flippantly, referred to,—which but a few days ago was the dream of her heart. Miss Lizzie, Miss Lizzie, all this strikes me as ethereal in the extreme ;—it looks to me as if you had been frightened into it ;—I fear you want to take back tracks from your excellent customer Mrs. Pelham !"

"Here are questions about Norman and Wales too," continued the reflective Superintendant. "Wonder if she was trying to startle Pelham into recognition, or confusion ? Wonder if she thought her an emissary of Wales, plotting to obtain for him the address of his confederate. Pelham has really done well in keeping her countenance through such an ordeal of surprises. But stay ;—I think I see it all now. One key only will unlock the whole mystery. Letter from Dudley sure enough—Delaney saw her read one. Let us suppose, —forger at last settled down,—apprehensive of his re-

treat being discovered,—even the name of the city or
state must be sacredly withheld,—only one dear sister-
in-law knows it,—warns her against all approach from
male or female inquisitors,—and dear little sister-in-law,
becoming frightened at having made a confidant, tries
to undo the effect of her own revelations. Clearly,
Miss Lizzie, that's just where we are."

From these reflections of the General Superintendent resulted two further inferences : First, that Dudley
had not left Boston, or at least its vicinity ; and second,
that we should scarcely ever learn from Lizzie precisely
where he was. Everything in her previous intercourse
with Mrs. Pelham had gone to show that she told the
natural truth, so far as that truth went. Everything in
this latest interview gave evidence of premeditation, and
a design to mislead. Either the girl had been strongly
cautioned, or of herself became alarmed at her impru-
dent confidences,—and whichever way we looked at it,
it seemed certain she would not repeat them.

Such, indeed, proved to be the case. Three or four
days afterwards Mrs. Pelham found a chance to let her
see the letter of the afflicted Mrs. White, and apparently
it brought Lizzie some mental comfort,—as if she had
been led to mistrust every movement of her friend.
But withal she did not speak further of Etta unless
when strongly constrained, and only a few casual refer-
ences were made to the couple that had removed so
suddenly from Boston to New York.

Once, indeed, in alluding to them, she accidentally mentioned them as living in Boston,—then she blushed, stammered, and quickly corrected herself by substituting New York. Mrs. Pelham did not pretend to notice either the blunder or its correction; though together they affirmed clearly that the Superintendant was right in both his conclusions.

The lady herself, indeed, attained to similar convictions by a different process of logic, which had the advantage of being founded on actual observation. In one of her last reports she expressed the belief that Miss Greenleaf had already confided to her all she knew of Dudley or his whereabouts, and all that she would under any circumstances confide to any one. "I am surprised even," added Mrs. Pelham, "that Lizzie ever told me thus much, for I know she is not by disposition a communicative girl, and no doubt she has now written to Dudley about me, and is acting under the forger's instructions."

Meanwhile Messrs. Thomas and Loomis had been actively engaged in the search for the outlaw. Although the Pittsburger had failed to identify Goodhue, the possibility that he might have forgotten his man, or be associating the name of Dudley with a different individual, inspired us to send on to Salem some other person who had known the forger. For this purpose we selected Mr. Grattan, the printer, introduced to my readers in the early part of this narrative, when Dudley as Cone, was planning his forgeries in Philadelphia; This gentleman accordingly went to Salem, and under direction of Mr. Thomas procured an interview with Goodhue, the detective himself being conveniently nigh at hand. The result was no better than before. Goodhue was not Cone, and therefore not Dudley.

It would far exceed the limits of this work if I were to chronicle in detail the search conducted by Thomas in Boston and its suburbs. It was continued day after day with unabated zeal and unflinching perseverance, until not only the city but every suburb within a dozen miles around had been thoroughly well ransacked. With the insurance agent it did wonders as a muscular training; for before many days were over he could walk his fifteen hours a day without a murmur or a groan.

But they found no Dudley—no forger.

* * *

CHAPTER XXXVI.

Risking much to Gain much.—Mr. Pinkerton orders a bold move.— Some peculiar Telegrams.—The wary little Clerk falls a Vic- tim to the new Stratagems.—And the assumed Name of the forger is at last Secured.

AT this time I was at my Chicago headquarters after a hard winter's work. During the progress of this case I had brought to an issue other operations of no less magnitude. With the first breath of summer, I was now longing for an interval of rest—for a change, be it ever so brief, from the ceaseless grind of duty, to the refreshing indolence of a "spell in the country." And only he, be it said, who toils with brain and pen in the choking atmosphere of a city office, can realize what a blessing it is to run riot for a while in the flowered prairies and blossom-scented woods of Central Illinois. There are stores of fresh vigor for him in every passing breeze—cordials of renovation in every wafted perfume.

But looking over these disheartening, interminable Dudley reports, I was almost in despair. When would this operation be at an end?—when should I get my coveted holiday?—for take it I would not with the case in suspense.

"Here we are," I reflected, "and the summer is almost with us; Mrs. Pelham is in Pittsburg at the very end of her string; Thomas lingers in Boston, trailing along a string that has no end; and meanwhile the Post-Office authorities want Wales, the Express Company is getting impatient, and Dudley is still at large, with all the world before him where to choose. It will certainly never do to fight it out on this line all summer. We must have a bolder policy—risk much to gain much,—and that without any delay."

Conformably to this determination I telegraphed to my General Superintendent the outline of a plan, which

will be best explained by its own working in the next
few pages. As the basis of its feasibility I assumed
very little beyond two facts : first—that the forger was
in Boston or its vicinity ; and second—that Miss Greenleaf had continued in correspondence with her sister,
Dudley's wife. If our efforts thus far had verified no
other conclusions, these they had beyond all manner of
doubt.

Monday morning following,—as the first move in
the new programme,—there arrived in the city of Pittsburg another of our detectives, Mr. Delaney having been
recalled a week or so before. To this officer, Mr. J. C.
Gabe, Mrs. Pelham had been directed to point out Miss
Greenleaf at the first opportunity, either by bringing
her out to the show window of the store, or in some
other effectual way. Thenceforth it became the duty
of Mr. Gabe to shadow every movement of Lizzie ;
and wherever she went, to see her persistently to her
destination, telegraphing the Agency on every unwonted
step. In certain contingencies, which he was informed
might arise after Wednesday morning, the detective had
certain instructions of a special nature.

In compliance with the above programme, the
"spot" on Miss Greenleaf was duly obtained on Monday afternoon ; and on that and the following day Mr.
Gabe saw her to and from Dunstable's as Delaney had
done for several weeks before. There was this difference now, however, that Lizzie, having removed into

the country with her grandmother, to see her to the train which bore her nightly from Pittsburg was equivalent to seeing her safely home. On the Wednesday morning, after shadowing her for the second time from the depot to the store, Mr. Gabe remained near the latter on vigilant guard.

Punctually at nine o'clock on the same Wednesday morning, Mr. Thomas despatched from Boston the following telegram.

"Miss Lizzie Greenleaf,

at Messrs. Dunstable Bros., Pittsburg.

"Husband badly hurt on cars. Come on at once. Will meet you at depot. Answer as before. Paid here.

"Etta."

The detective who launched out this decoy had also his instructions of a contingent character. I had calculated that on the delivery of the message to Miss Greenleaf one or more of three events would follow: she would in all probability send a telegraphic reply: she would also be likely to mail a letter to her sister; —and she might, either immediately or within a day or two, proceed in person to Boston. This last course would, to us, have been the most acceptable of all; as it must have led our shadows direct, and with the least loss of time, to the forger's hiding-place. Precisely what did happen will now appear.

In Pittsburg it was about half past ten o'clock when Mr. Gabe saw the telegraph messenger entering Dunstable's store. This was one of the contingencies for which he had been prepared,—in fact, he already knew what the telegram was, and for whom intended. But nothing now could be left to mere hap-hazard;—every step and circumstance must be assured and verified.

In the space of about half a minute the detective passed slowly by the door, and with a sweeping glance inward observed at a rear counter Miss Greenleaf reading the dispatch, and the boy standing by as if waiting for the answer. Turning on his heel immediately Gabe went into the store, and engaged one of the assistants near the front with some aimless inquiries, just long enough to perceive that Lizzie was writing a message at the book-keeper's desk, and the telegraph boy seated, evidently waiting to take charge of it. Without losing another moment the detective was again in the street, and watching at a little distance for the lad to come forth.

In due time the messenger stepped out, with the freshly-written paper folded into his dispatch book.

Now, indeed, had come the crowning emergency, —to the detective, to Bangs, to myself, to all of us ;—for in that dispatch of Miss Greenleaf must be the forger's address !

The boy at once took the direction of the telegraph

station—which was distant about four blocks—but
with that listless indifference to haste which is a characteristic of youths of his profession. When about two
blocks of the way he was overtaken by a staid, clerkly-
looking man, without any hat, and with a pen project-
ing over his ear, who tapped him on the shoulder, and
somewhat breathlessly demanded:

"Say, bub, it's you that's just been in Dunstable's?"

"Yessir, that's me."

"I'm so glad I overtook you. Miss Greenleaf left
out a word in that message she has just given you, and
she hurried me after you to stick it in. Lady couldn't
run out of the store herself, you know."

"Bub" looked, and listened, and hesitated,—and
with a dim consciousness of his exact duty seemed in
clined to go back to the lady herself.

"Here,—you know I'm the book-keeper at Dunstable's,—she gave me this quarter dollar for you, so that
you shouldn't delay; take this pencil and write the
word in yourself—I'll show you where,—it will answer
just the same."

Thus appealed to the boy no longer resisted, and at
once spread the paper out on the cover of his book, so
that Mr. Gabe,—for he was the pretended book-keeper,
—could point out where the word was wanting. There
being already ten words in the message the only one
the officer could suggest was the word "Greenleaf,"

"Say bub, is it you that's just been in Dunstable's?"

which he caused the lad to write after the "Lizzie" with which the dispatch was signed.

"You see," he said, complacently, as he left the boy to proceed, "they mightn't think who it was from unless Miss Greenleaf wrote her full name."

Brief as his opportunity was, the detective had time enough to commit to memory the address and contents of the telegram, which were as follows:

"MRS. E. H. PURCELL,
                    Boston, Mass.

"Cannot possibly go. Marcella sick. Alone in country with Grandmamma.

                              "LIZZIE."

Donning the soft hat which he now took out of his pocket, Mr. Gabe hastened to another telegraph station, and after transmitting Lizzie's telegram to the Agency, returned at once to his post near Dunstable's. At noon Miss Greenleaf left the store as usual, and hurriedly proceeded to her sister's house in Alleghany City. Here she spent the greater part of an hour, and on her return dropped a letter into a street postal-box, and next went into a telegraph station and forwarded another dispatch.

What either of these contained, of course, Gabe had no means of knowing, but according to his instructions he again telegraphed the facts. Once more he resumed his watch until evening; saw Miss Greenleaf to the Cumberland Valley Railroad, and into the train that was to carry her to her country home; and then remained at the depot until such late hour that he knew she could not again get to Pittsburg before morning.

On his return to the hotel Gabe found awaiting him a dispatch from Mr. Bangs, cautioning him that Lizzie had said in her second dispatch that she might yet go East. He was therefore to continue on his shadow duty until further orders,—being ready at all moments to jump on the same train with her if she left the city.

Mrs. Pelham had been notified to continue as if nothing happened, but be keenly on the alert if Lizzie should again express willingness to go to Boston; proposing to accompany her if it could be done without exciting suspicion.

We must now rejoin Mr. Thomas at Boston, if we would see what had been gained by his startling telegram of the morning. About an hour after noon he received a dispatch from Mr. Linden, telling him that Lizzie had sent a reply addressed to Mrs. E. H. Purcell, and that it was to be procured at the telegraph office under that name. This he found it easy to do by means of a written order purporting to be from that lady, and all the easier that he was himself known as the person who

telegraphed in the morning to Miss Greenleaf of Pittsburg.

Before three o'clock he had another telegram in
forming him that Lizzie had sent a second dispatch,
which he was to obtain in like manner, and telegraph
a copy back to the New York Agency, where its contents were as yet unknown. In this also he was successful, the dispatch so obtained and re-transmitted
being as follows:

" Mrs. E. H. Purcell,

Boston, Massachusetts.

" May come later, but would not know where to go.
See to-day's letter.

" Lizzie."

This latter, it will be seen, was the telegram which
Lizzie forwarded on her way to the store from Alleghany City, and the letter referred to in it, the letter
she had then mailed. It was also the inspiration of the
Agency telegram which Mr. Gabe received late at night,
directing him to stand by his post on the chance of
Lizzie taking train for the East.

Now, if anything was clear from these two telegrams
of Lizzie, it was that Dudley was using the name of
Mrs. E. H. Purcell as a cover for his correspondence,
and that this address—incomplete as it was—had already
sufficed to bring his sister-in-law's letters to him. If she
were possessed of a more detailed one, she would cer-

tainly use it for her telegrams in this hour of calamity ; and indeed the second dispatch proved beyond doubt that she did not know of any, and that Dudley had never confided to her his exact whereabouts in Boston. After all, the girl had told Mrs. Pelham the truth ; and excepting the protective name of Purcell, we really knew as much a month before, as by stratagem we had now learned.

But this name was everything. Thomas did not need to wait for instructions to betake himself at once to the General Delivery room at the post-office, and there to watch—with Loomis in the near neighborhood— for the person who might call for a letter for Mrs. E. H. Purcell. Whether rarely or frequently, it was evident that this was the only place at which the forger could obtain letters so indefinitely addressed.

CHAPTER XXXVII.

The Net drawing closer and closer around the Criminal.—Prepara-
tions for Dudley's Reception at the Boston Post-office.—The
final Capture of the Forger.—A simple Device discloses his
Residence and recovers the Plunder.—The End.

MR. BANGS now decided to make a trip to Boston. He felt that the conclusion of the operation was now at hand, and that fitting arrangements should be made on the field of battle. Everything had been staked for an early triumph; and the smallest hitch or misconstruction might shatter all our plans. Neither to the mail or the telegraph, therefore, would he intrust those final instructions on which the victorious issue depended.

Starting from New York in the afternoon he found Mr. Thomas shortly before midnight in the Sherman House, in Boston. The detective was better pleased to see him than a dozen letters, for he was not a little oppressed with the responsibility of his mission, and naturally felt relieved when under the guidance of his sagacious chief.

"Has Miss Greenleaf's letter arrived?" was the first question of the General Superintendent, as soon as they were closeted safe from intrusion.

"It has, sir;—it is now in the post-office," replied the detective.

"How?—In the General Delivery office?"

"Yes; it is assorted with the other letters under the initial, P."

"How have you learned this?"

"Well, this morning I prepared a written order in a woman's handwriting —signed, of course, for Mrs. E. H. Purcell,—and presented myself at the delivery window, asking for that lady's letters. The clerk took down all the mail matter in the box P., and running over the letters, handed me one so addressed. I saw that it had the Pittsburg postmark on, and was mailed yesterday."

"Then I walked a few steps away from the window, and returned again with the letter to the clerk, saying: 'This is a mistake, sir; there must be another Mrs. E. H. Purcell,—my sister has no correspondent in Pittsburg.' He took back the letter from me, and I saw him replace it in the same box."

"Good; we are now entirely certain that Lizzie has used that address before, and that Dudley either comes or sends for the letters of his wife. Can you see this box P from the hall outside?"

"Oh! quite well;—there is a glass partition through which all the alphabetical boxes are plainly visible."

"Is there anything externally striking about Miss Greenleaf's letter?"

"No, sir; it has a common buff envelope, like hundreds of others."

"How near can you stand to the delivery window without being in the way of traffic, and at the same time without appearing to watch it?"

"I should say from four to eight yards."

"So that if a boy, or a strange woman," pursued Mr. Bangs, "were to call for Mrs. Purcell's letter, you could scarcely tell when it was handed out?"

"Not very well, sir,—or not at all, perhaps, without going close to the railing, and hearing the person apply for it."

" It will never do to rely on that," said Mr. Bangs, seriously; " we must know beyond peradventure the very moment that letter is called for. If it gets out without our knowledge, all is lost; for Dudley will take immediate flight on learning that snares are being laid in Boston for him."

After a brief interval of reflection he next inquired of Thomas if any registered letters were delivered at that window, and what was the process?

" It would seem," replied the detective, "that very few registered letters are addressed to the General Delivery at all; and when there are any, they are not kept there. Instead of that, I find that a red card with the same address is put into the proper box, and takes its place with the letters under the same initial. Then, when the owner appears, this card is given to him, and he takes it to the Registered Letter department, where he is expected to prove his identity, and sign the receipt for his letter."

" I presume you have seen some of those red cards handed out?"

" Only one during the entire day," was the reply of Thomas, "nor did I observe another in any of the boxes."

" If there were any of them, I suppose you could discern them from the outside?"

" All the time, sir; the card could be distinguished twenty yards away."

This was precisely what was wanted. The Superintendent now directed Mr. Thomas to register and mail, the first thing in the morning, a decoy envelope addressed to Mrs. E. H. Purcell, as for the General Delivery. This would have the effect of placing in the box P a red card with the same name on it; and as long as there were anything with that address, so conspicuous that it could not be passed out without Thomas seeing it, he must infallibly know when the Pittsburg letter was applied for—both being certain to be handed down to the applicant. As a further precaution, however, he was also to mail for her a very large, tinted envelope, which he would be enabled to see in the box at all times, and to miss on the moment of its removal.

Learning further from the detective that the business of the General Delivery was transacted for twelve hours daily—from 7.30 A. M. to 7.30 P. M.—Mr. Bangs at once telegraphed to New York for Officer Delaney to come on to Boston. To him was to be assigned the task of relieving Mr. Thomas at meal times, and of taking an occasional spell of the watch, should other clues demand the attention of Thomas. Mr. Loomis was also to have his part in this ambush, to the extent of waiting near at hand to identify the forger, but he was never to loiter round the post-office unless in disguise, and as little as possible even in the streets of the city. Telling Thomas he would call on him next forenoon at his post of duty, the superintendent then retired for his much-needed rest.

In the morning Mr. Bangs visited the Postmaster of Boston, and informing him that we were in pursuit of a noted law-breaker, who would call at the General Delivery office for letters, requested permission for our detectives to remain around the building so long as their watch might be necessary. The official readily consented, and gave the needful orders to the chief janitor, that Mr. Thomas and his associate should be spared all notice or interference. He further graciously suggested —on learning that the criminal was associated with mail robbers—that the office of the Special Agent, within the building, might be used as a rendezvous should occasion require it.

Shortly before noon the General Superintendent called on Mr. Thomas, and found that attentive individual in the corridor of the post-office, watching keenly towards the delivery window through which Mrs. Purcell's letter must pass. Through the glass partition the detective pointed out to him the alphabet boxes, and in the compartment " P " a large green-tinted envelope and a registered letter card, both shoved in alongside the pile of ordinary-sized epistles that were classed under this letter. From the spot where they stood, and for a short distance either way, the removal of these objects by the clerk could be instantaneously perceived.

"That green one is our display letter," observed

Mr. Thomas, "and the card next to it is the registered letter ticket."

"Keep a good eye on them," said Mr. Bangs, encouragingly, "you will have Delaney with you from to-night. If Dudley himself comes to the trap, be prompt as thought, and take no nonsense whatever from him; if it be a woman or other messenger, shadow them out very cautiously and they will undoubtedly lead you to your man."

Before leaving Boston that night the General Superintendent gave further and fuller instructions to Thomas about the arrest of Dudley. At my suggestion he also telegraphed to Lizzie Greenleaf in the following words:

'Husband better. Shall write soon.

"ETTA."

It being evident that we were now as near to Dudley as the girl herself could get by coming to Boston, there seemed to me no occasion for prolonging the disquietude which the first dispatch might have caused to her. It would also result that the further presence of Mr. Gabe in Pittsburg could be dispensed with.

The only weak spot in our armor now, was, that Dudley might write to his sister-in-law a letter which would show that she had been played upon. Of this we were scarcely apprehensive, however, for Lizzie herself had told us that the forger was the last who wrote, —or anyhow, his wife,—and it was much more likely

he would first call at the post-office for the answer to
their letter. For the rest, we would depend on Mrs.
Pelham, who was more than ever in the good graces of
Lizzie, and would perceive promptly any symptoms
that might betoken a collapse.

Day after day the watch of Mr. Thomas now continued. Even when Delaney was on hand he would
scarcely leave the post-office except for a hasty dinner.
He was so certain that he would recognize Dudley,
while Delaney might not, that in very eagerness he assumed the lion's share of the duty. He watched the delivery window and its visitors with the eye of a lynx.
The green-tinted envelope and the red ticket seared
themselves into his brain as the tokens of approaching
triumph. Even in his dreams he did not cease to behold them, glaring nebulously from a shadowy letter-
box, or handed by a spectral mail-clerk to some phan-
tasmal Dudley!

On several occasions men called for letters who
bore a general resemblance to the forger; but eager and
impatient as he was, Thomas did not rush into blunders.
Prompted every night by the friendly Loomis, and sat-
urated with descriptions, verbal and written, he had so
"figured down" the identity of Dudley that the smallest of his peculiarities would have been apprehended
or missed.

Several times also when letters were applied for
from the same compartment, the delivery clerk would
14*

take down and glance at the red ticket, and the big eccentric envelope. They were never brought to the window, though, and had merely been examined to refresh a laggard memory. By and by they remained altogether undisturbed, as if both the clerks at the delivery desk had become familiar with their superscription.

On Sundays there was but a single hour of this watch duty, and the detectives spent the remainder of the day patrolling Boston and its suburbs, in hopes to meet Dudley, or get a glimpse of the brass canary cage. In the evenings, too, they visited theaters and resorts innumerable, hoping to discover him among the votaries of pleasure. But all these various researches were as fruitless as ever.

Thus the time passed until the thirtieth of May. Thomas had been at his post as usual from the opening of the office. Delaney was within hail, but a little way retired. Neither expected anything else than another long day of monotonous vigilance.

About half-past ten o'clock on this morning, a gentleman stepped briskly up to the delivery window whose appearance caused an unwonted flutter in the pulse of Thomas. He could not be mistaken—every lineament was there—every feature and peculiarity were in accord with his mental portraiture;—this must be none other than the forger himself!

As Thomas walked over to him, the man had already asked for letters for Mrs. E. H. Purcell, and was being

The detective at once arrested him as Robert L. Dudley.

informed by the clerk about the registered letter, which the ticket would enable him to claim in the proper department. Lizzie Greenleaf's letter was in his possession, however, and that was enough for Thomas. Laying his hand on his shoulder, the detective at once arrested him as Robert L. Dudley, forger of a certain draft in the City of Pittsburg, Commonwealth of Pennsylvania.

The criminal behaved with great coolness and self-possession. He stared out a well-affected astonishment, and gently protested that his name was not Dudley, but Rathbun, and he could prove it quite readily.

"Step this way, Mr. Rathbun, and let us see," replied the phlegmatic Thomas, not for a moment doubting however, that he had nabbed the right man.

Beckoning to Delaney, the detective at once took him into the office of Special Agent Fields, where he left him in charge of his companion, while he ran to the Sherman House to bring Loomis to the spot.

In a very brief space the Pittsburger arrived at the post-office, and in the most positive manner identified the prisoner as Dudley. The latter affected not to know him, and bravely endeavored to carry out his role of injured innocence. Thomas, however, immediately slipped handcuffs on him, and proceeded to search his pockets, finding therein only the unopened letters, about fifty dollars in money, and a few personal trifles of no consequence. He also had some railway tickets from Boston to Mattapan, a quiet little village some miles from the city.

As it had been ascertained from Wales that Dudley must be possessed of some nine or ten thousand dollars, usually secured on his wife's person, it became important to arrest her and obtain this money before it could be made away with. As a bait in that direction, Thomas now impressed upon him that he must start for Pittsburg with his custodians by the three o'clock train, but, if he wanted some changes of clothing, and was willing to pay for a hack to go after them, he would meanwhile be permitted to call at his home.

By this time the prisoner was completely crestfallen, and had confessed to Loomis that there was really no mistake, that he was the R. L. Dudley who had resided in Pittsburg. He now accepted the proposition of Thomas, and a carriage was called, into which he was taken by the officers. As might be presumed, he directed them to drive to Mattapan, and as soon as they had reached that suburb he was summoned to point out his abode. This he reluctantly did, and the carriage being stopped a short distance away, Thomas and Loomis went and rang the house-bell.

It was Lizzie Greenleaf's sister, in person, who opened the door; and stepping into the hall quickly the detective arrested her as an accomplice of the forger —explaining that the latter was outside, a manacled prisoner. The unfortunate woman was at first paralyzed

It was Lizzie Greenleaf's sister, in person, who opened the door.

with fright; but she soon recovered herself, and became cool as an old jail-bird.

To the demand for Dudley's money, which was now made on her, his wife responded very stubbornly, that she had none, and knew nothing of it. Unwilling to submit her to the indignity of a personal search, Thomas employed strategy to obtain it. Keeping her securely under his eye he whispered Loomis to go back to the carriage, and urge on the forger the degrading alternative to which his wife must be exposed if she persisted longer in her refusal.

The result might be anticipated. Loomis returned from Dudley with particulars of all the plunder and how it was distributed or concealed; with also a penciled message to his wife, that nothing was to be gained by any attempt to withhold it from the officers. Stepping to the hall-door by permission, she received a further sign from the carriage window that such indeed was her husband's conclusion.

Mrs. Dudley then yielded, and handed Mr. Thomas —principally from its concealment in her clothing— about six thousand dollars; of which amount half was in Government bonds, and the remainder in bills and other securities. She also surrendered the deed of the house and lot in which they were living, value for upwards of four thousand dollars more. The forger and his wife were then taken promptly to Boston, but in separate conveyances, each in charge of one of our two detectives. Before sundown Dudley was safe under bolt and bar in Suffolk street Jail ; and the lady was held under arrest in a room at the Sherman House.

Protracted as it had been, and often endangered, the issue of our operation was a complete triumph. Criminals and spoils were now alike in the hands of Justice ; and her vindication was assured under the laws of the land. The unconscious blotting-paper had achieved its mission as a detector. The clue in the mirror had led us safely to the end.

The remainder of my story may be briefly told, being merely that sequence of our operation which necessarily saw light in the public press.

The Adams' Express Company made an immediate attachment on the forger's property at Mattapan. With this, and the money obtained from Mrs. Dudley, as well as the plunder which had been previously disgorged by Wales, our employers were enable to reimburse themselves for their losses on the forged draft.

The prisoners were not at once taken West, but held for a few days until taken before a United States Commissioner. By this official Dudley was remanded for trial at Pittsburg ; whither he was then promptly sent and placed in jail.

As to his wife, the Express Company generously urged that she be no further molested. She had at one stroke lost husband, home and subsistence; and as in his person the outraged law would be amply avenged, it was agreed that her punishment had been already adequate.

Almost simultaneously with their arrest Mrs. Pelham had left Pittsburg—summoned to the bedside of a dying relative—nor am I aware that she has since revisited that city of dusky distinction.

To the great relief of Mr. Linden, as of myself, Wales was taken off our hands within a very few days, and committed by the United States authorities to the same ordeal, and in the same city, as Dudley.

But in good earnest the summer had now come. Dust and silence reigned in the temples of law, and judges and attorneys were enjoying themselves with rod and gun all over the broad land. It was not until the middle of the November following that the two criminals were tried before the United States Circuit Court, at Pittsburg. There was quite sufficient evidence for the conviction of both; but to the last Dudley refused all recognition of his former confederate in crime. In the grim solitude of his prison cell, however, he was heard to revile him bitterly; and to claim, with indignant oaths, that but for the infernal vanity and gasconade of Wales, their game of plunder would never have been discovered.

Be that as it may, they were both sentenced for a

like term to the Western Penitentiary, in Alleghany City, where they are still expiating their crimes by toiling under sentence of the law for the profit of the Commonwealth of Pennsylvania.